$3

This book belongs to

_____

Gratitude

Diary and Daily Planner

2011

Morthern Spears

First published in Australia in 2010 by Morthern Spears
PO Box 31, Ocean Shores, NSW 2483

Moon Guides copyright © Tess Cullen
The moon phases in this diary are correct for Australian Eastern Standard time (150E00). In America, England and Europe, due to time zone changes, the moon phase may occur on the previous day.

ISBN: 978-0-9805190-4-4

Photo credits

Cover:	**Tm J**
January:	**Joseph Kellard**
February:	**Marsel van Oosten**
March:	**Dave Barston**
April:	**Pavel Orlovski**
May:	**Adrian Pop**
June:	**Dariusz Wieclawski**
July:	**Bread and Shutter**
August:	**Mário Mat**
September:	**Claire Gray**
October:	**Umair Ghani**
November:	**Dieter Biskamp**
December:	**Andy Glogower**

The publisher would like to thank everyone who has given permission to use the quotes used in this diary. In some cases it has not been possible to contact the author/publisher of the quotes used and any information regarding the ownership of copyright is welcomed by the publisher.
A special thanks to:
Robert Brault /www.robertbrault.com
Daniel Ladinsky *The Subject Tonight is Love, 60 Wild & Sweet Poems of Hafiz*
Ramtha
Renee Searles *Lace Wings* 2009 www.myspace.com/reneesearles
A very special thanks to AJ Miller for unrestricted access and reproduction of his work.
www.divinetruth.com.au

Moon and Astrological guide by Tess Cullen, Byron Bay: www.tesscullen.com
Design: Best Legenz Pty Ltd: www.bestlegenz.com.au
Printed in China

Website, **www.diarygratitude.com**
Here you can reorder your diary for next year, make enquiries about becoming a distributor, share your experiences in the practice of gratitude and network with others on a similar path. Check it out !

Gratitude

Welcome to the 2011 Gratitude Diary and Daily Planner. This year, the theme is relationships. I have explored issues such as attraction, romance, love, soulmates and community. Remember, we all have relationships with people all the time, so consider the quotes in relation to not just one significant other, but to many.

Occasionally, I have added a prompt in the journaling section, a question or a statement to provoke your own enquiry. It is wonderful to be grateful, no doubt. However, it is also necessary to ponder, re-evaluate, and desire. For without desire, what are we creating for ourselves and our futures?

You may also notice my new preoccupation with God. I am coming to desire a deeper connection to truth, and this guy just keeps showing up!

Sometimes I have quoted from the Bible, Jesus, or from ascended entities no longer living on this plane. No matter what the source, there is no religious intent in any of the verses. If you feel yourself becoming reactive to what has been suggested, this is a wonderful opportunity to journal your thoughts and feelings, and to feel them!

I'm more interested in what God's messages to us are and desire that each and every one of us (including myself) are conscious enough to feel his truth, irrespective of religion, race, culture, beliefs or conditioning.

Who knows what the state of the world will be like in futures near? So remember, if all else is failing in your life, there is always God.

love Morthern

The Solar Lunar Cycles or Lunar Phases

The cyclic relationship between the Sun, the Moon and the Earth symbolises our spiritually driven journey in all its stages. The sun represents the masculine outpouring of the vital, ever-present spirit whilst the moon represents the feminine inward all knowing memories and cycles of our soul. The Sun inspires and the Moon embodies, equally active in this dance of life. Each cycle grows from a place of quiet emptiness, into ideas that become actions and then produce a visible experience-which is then distributed and reassessed before returning to the void to begin again.

The cycle begins deep in the bowels of the feminine with the Dark Moon, a time of devoted to inwardness, the still point between breaths. We are pulsed by the cosmic consciousness during the meditative flavour of this phase. In the first glimmer of the New Moon ideas stir and growth begins. A multitude of possibilities flourish as new inspirations prosper. The impulses that take root are the seedlings of the next adventures entering your life.

*In this waxing phase, the **First Quarter** erupts into a time of action where ideas/visions become reality. The waiting is over. It is time to GO! That which has only been a thought becomes manifest and, with effort and commitment to the new impulses, projects take root. There is much support and more interaction with those around us.*

*The **Full Moon** is a time to dance in the light, to be out and on show for all to see. This is the brightest phase of the cycle, where we can see what we are doing. There's no holding back, it is the time to be utterly involved in life, people and projects. As the moon begins to wane we begin to wind down yet there is still a lot of work to be done. We review, revise and demonstrate to others what we have learnt or experienced.*

*The **Last Quarter** brings change, we seek to understand the picture that is bigger than our current experience. We begin to pack up in order to either store or give away our knowledge, possessions or experiences. The search for a greater purpose is renewed.*

*As we approach the **Dark Moon** whatever is not in harmony with our consciousness must be repudiated. Expand into a world where the experience sought is other than the mundane material reality; surrender, for a while, into the vast emptiness of the divine unknowing.*

TESS CULLEN is a professional astrologer, teacher and writer who readily shares her knowledge. She holds a Dip Astro (FAA—Federation of Australian Astrologers) and Dip Ancient & Medieval Studies (Astrologos), is a current member of the FAA and APA (Assoc of Professional Astrologers) and has a practice in Byron Bay, Northern NSW. www.tesscullen.com

Personal Details

Important information

Name _____

Address _____

_____

Home Phone _____

Work Phone _____

Mobile _____

Email _____

Business information

Tax file number _____

Licence _____

Passport number _____

ABN _____

Other _____

Medical instructions

Blood type _____

Allergies _____

Doctor _____

In case of illness contact

Name _____

Address _____

_____

Phone _____

Mobile _____

2011 Yearly Planner

January	February	March
1	1	1
2	2	2
3	3	3
4	4	4
5	5	5
6	6	6
7	7	7
8	8	8
9	9	9
10	10	10
11	11	11
12	12	12
13	13	13
14	14	14
15	15	15
16	16	16
17	17	17
18	18	18
19	19	19
20	20	20
21	21	21
22	22	22
23	23	23
24	24	24
25	25	25
26	26	26
27	27	27
28	28	28
29		29
30		30
31		31

2011 Yearly Planner

April	May	June
1 _____	1 _____	1 _____
2 _____	2 _____	2 _____
3 _____	3 _____	3 _____
4 _____	4 _____	4 _____
5 _____	5 _____	5 _____
6 _____	6 _____	6 _____
7 _____	7 _____	7 _____
8 _____	8 _____	8 _____
9 _____	9 _____	9 _____
10 _____	10 _____	10 _____
11 _____	11 _____	11 _____
12 _____	12 _____	12 _____
13 _____	13 _____	13 _____
14 _____	14 _____	14 _____
15 _____	15 _____	15 _____
16 _____	16 _____	16 _____
17 _____	17 _____	17 _____
18 _____	18 _____	18 _____
19 _____	19 _____	19 _____
20 _____	20 _____	20 _____
21 _____	21 _____	21 _____
22 _____	22 _____	22 _____
23 _____	23 _____	23 _____
24 _____	24 _____	24 _____
25 _____	25 _____	25 _____
26 _____	26 _____	26 _____
27 _____	27 _____	27 _____
28 _____	28 _____	28 _____
29 _____	29 _____	29 _____
30 _____	30 _____	30 _____
	31 _____	

2011 Yearly Planner

July	August	September
1 _____	1 _____	1 _____
2 _____	2 _____	2 _____
3 _____	3 _____	3 _____
4 _____	4 _____	4 _____
5 _____	5 _____	5 _____
6 _____	6 _____	6 _____
7 _____	7 _____	7 _____
8 _____	8 _____	8 _____
9 _____	9 _____	9 _____
10 _____	10 _____	10 _____
11 _____	11 _____	11 _____
12 _____	12 _____	12 _____
13 _____	13 _____	13 _____
14 _____	14 _____	14 _____
15 _____	15 _____	15 _____
16 _____	16 _____	16 _____
17 _____	17 _____	17 _____
18 _____	18 _____	18 _____
19 _____	19 _____	19 _____
20 _____	20 _____	20 _____
21 _____	21 _____	21 _____
22 _____	22 _____	22 _____
23 _____	23 _____	23 _____
24 _____	24 _____	24 _____
25 _____	25 _____	25 _____
26 _____	26 _____	26 _____
27 _____	27 _____	27 _____
28 _____	28 _____	28 _____
29 _____	29 _____	29 _____
30 _____	30 _____	30 _____
31 _____	31 _____	

2011 Yearly Planner

October	November	December
1 _____	1 _____	1 _____
2 _____	2 _____	2 _____
3 _____	3 _____	3 _____
4 _____	4 _____	4 _____
5 _____	5 _____	5 _____
6 _____	6 _____	6 _____
7 _____	7 _____	7 _____
8 _____	8 _____	8 _____
9 _____	9 _____	9 _____
10 _____	10 _____	10 _____
11 _____	11 _____	11 _____
12 _____	12 _____	12 _____
13 _____	13 _____	13 _____
14 _____	14 _____	14 _____
15 _____	15 _____	15 _____
16 _____	16 _____	16 _____
17 _____	17 _____	17 _____
18 _____	18 _____	18 _____
19 _____	19 _____	19 _____
20 _____	20 _____	20 _____
21 _____	21 _____	21 _____
22 _____	22 _____	22 _____
23 _____	23 _____	23 _____
24 _____	24 _____	24 _____
25 _____	25 _____	25 _____
26 _____	26 _____	26 _____
27 _____	27 _____	27 _____
28 _____	28 _____	28 _____
29 _____	29 _____	29 _____
30 _____	30 _____	30 _____
31 _____		31 _____

Desire

In the receiving of Divine Love, there are three principals to remember:

1. Have a soul longing for God's Love to enter you

2. Deeply Desire the Divine Truth to enter you, which is also God's truth

3. Be Humble with a passionate Desire to experience your own emotions

AJ Miller

January

Photo by Joseph Kellard

January 2011

Monday	Tuesday	Wednesday	Thursday	Friday	Saturday	Sunday
				1	2	
3	4	5	6	7	8	9
10	11	12	13	14	15	16
17	18	19	20	21	22	23
24	25	26	27	28	29	30
31						

Today I am Grateful for . . .

_____
_____
_____
_____
_____
_____
_____

Saturday 1 January

_____
_____
_____
_____
_____
_____
_____
_____
_____

Sunday 2 January

_____
_____
_____
_____
_____
_____
_____
_____
_____

Today I am Grateful for ...

_____

_____

_____

_____

_____

_____

Monday 3 January

8 am

_____

10 am

_____

12 pm

_____

2 pm

_____

4 pm

_____

6 pm

_____

Once we ourselves progress in love, we come to see that there is a vast difference between neediness and love, and there is a large difference between need and desire. Need is usually based around emotional injuries, while love is driven by pure and sincere passion or desire.

AJ Miller

		December 2010				
M	T	W	T	F	S	S
		1	2	3	4	5
6	7	8	9	10	11	12
13	14	15	16	17	18	19
20	21	22	23	24	25	26
27	28	29	30	31		

Today I am Grateful for . . .

○

Tuesday 4 January

8 am

New or Dark Moon in Capricorn **Solar Eclipse (partial) 13° Capricorn**
Each Lunar Cycle begins with the monthly New Moon and when combined with a Solar Eclipse the impact is stronger on our collective psyche. The foundations that underlay our culture have ancient roots and are being challenged to reframe and keep what is functional whilst allowing space for newer brighter ideas to emerge. The choices made now have long-lasting effects.

10 am

12 pm

2 pm

4 pm

6 pm

February 2011

M	T	W	T	F	S	S
	1	2	3	4	5	6
7	8	9	10	11	12	13
14	15	16	17	18	19	20
21	22	23	24	25	26	27
28						

Today I am Grateful for . . .

_____

_____

_____

_____

_____

Wednesday 5 January

8 am

10 am

12 pm

2 pm

4 pm

6 pm

December 2010

M	T	W	T	F	S	S
		1	2	3	4	5
6	7	8	9	10	11	12
13	14	15	16	17	18	19
20	21	22	23	24	25	26
27	28	29	30	31		

I deeply Desire . . .

_____

_____

_____

_____

_____

_____

Thursday 6 January

8 am

_____

_____

10 am

_____

_____

12 pm

_____

_____

2 pm

_____

_____

4 pm

_____

_____

6 pm

_____

_____

February 2011

M	T	W	T	F	S	S
	1	2	3	4	5	6
7	8	9	10	11	12	13
14	15	16	17	18	19	20
21	22	23	24	25	26	27
28						

Today I am Grateful for . . .

_____
_____
_____
_____
_____
_____

Friday 7 January

8 am
_____
_____

10 am
_____
_____

12 pm
_____
_____

2 pm
_____
_____

4 pm
_____
_____

6 pm
_____
_____

December 2010

M	T	W	T	F	S	S
		1	2	3	4	5
6	7	8	9	10	11	12
13	14	15	16	17	18	19
20	21	22	23	24	25	26
27	28	29	30	31		

Do I feel that God Desires my Love?

Saturday 8 January

Sunday 9 January

Today I am Grateful for . . .

_____
_____
_____
_____
_____
_____

Monday 10 January

8 am
_____
_____

10 am
_____
_____

12 pm
_____
_____

2 pm
_____
_____

4 pm
_____
_____

6 pm
_____
_____

Manifest plainness,
Embrace simplicity,
Reduce selfishness,
Have few desires.

Lao-tzu

December 2010

M	T	W	T	F	S	S
		1	2	3	4	5
6	7	8	9	10	11	12
13	14	15	16	17	18	19
20	21	22	23	24	25	26
27	28	29	30	31		

Today I am Grateful for . . .

_____
_____
_____
_____
_____
_____

Tuesday 11 January

8 am
_____
_____

10 am
_____
_____

12 pm
_____
_____

2 pm
_____
_____

4 pm
_____
_____

6 pm
_____
_____

February 2011						
M	T	W	T	F	S	S
	1	2	3	4	5	6
7	8	9	10	11	12	13
14	15	16	17	18	19	20
21	22	23	24	25	26	27
28						

Today I am Grateful for ...

_____
_____
_____
_____
_____

First Quarter Waxing Moon in Aries
Integrity is where we find the balance between our inner and outer world,
the place of clarity in all our choices. A time to act upon decisions that are
in line with your personal integrity.

Wednesday 12 January

8 am
_____

10 am
_____

12 pm
_____

2 pm
_____

4 pm
_____

6 pm
_____

		December 2010				
M	T	W	T	F	S	S
		1	2	3	4	5
6	7	8	9	10	11	12
13	14	15	16	17	18	19
20	21	22	23	24	25	26
27	28	29	30	31		

Today I am Grateful for . . .

Thursday 13 January

8 am

---

10 am

---

12 pm

---

2 pm

---

4 pm

---

6 pm

February 2011

M	T	W	T	F	S	S
	1	2	3	4	5	6
7	8	9	10	11	12	13
14	15	16	17	18	19	20
21	22	23	24	25	26	27
28						

Today I am Desiring . . .

_____
_____
_____
_____
_____
_____

Friday 14 January

8 am
_____
_____

10 am
_____
_____

12 pm
_____
_____

2 pm
_____
_____

4 pm
_____
_____

6 pm
_____
_____

December 2010						
M	T	W	T	F	S	S
		1	2	3	4	5
6	7	8	9	10	11	12
13	14	15	16	17	18	19
20	21	22	23	24	25	26
27	28	29	30	31		

Today I am Grateful for . . .

Saturday 15 January

Sunday 16 January

Today I am Grateful for . . .

_____
_____
_____
_____
_____

Monday 17 January

8 am
_____
_____

10 am
_____
_____

12 pm
_____
_____

2 pm
_____
_____

4 pm
_____
_____

6 pm
_____
_____

The desire of the man is for the woman, but the desire of the woman is for the desire of the man.

Madame de Stael

December 2010

M	T	W	T	F	S	S
		1	2	3	4	5
6	7	8	9	10	11	12
13	14	15	16	17	18	19
20	21	22	23	24	25	26
27	28	29	30	31		

Today I am Grateful for . . .

_____

_____

_____

_____

_____

_____

_____

Tuesday 18 January

8 am

_____

_____

10 am

_____

_____

12 pm

_____

_____

2 pm

_____

_____

4 pm

_____

_____

6 pm

_____

_____

February 2011

M	T	W	T	F	S	S
	1	2	3	4	5	6
7	8	9	10	11	12	13
14	15	16	17	18	19	20
21	22	23	24	25	26	27
28						

I Deeply want . . .

_____
_____
_____
_____
_____
_____

Wednesday 19 January

8 am
_____
_____

10 am
_____
_____

12 pm
_____
_____

2 pm
_____
_____

4 pm
_____
_____

6 pm
_____
_____

December 2010						
M	T	W	T	F	S	S
		1	2	3	4	5
6	7	8	9	10	11	12
13	14	15	16	17	18	19
20	21	22	23	24	25	26
27	28	29	30	31		

Today I am Grateful for . . .

_____

_____

_____

_____

_____

_____

_____

Thursday 20 January

Full Moon in Cancer
Get ready! Forces of change are affecting the world and restructuring the current belief systems. As we await the birth of a new paradigm, remember there is still time to clean out the cupboard of the old unnecessary stuff.

8 am

10 am

12 pm

2 pm

4 pm

6 pm

February 2011

M	T	W	T	F	S	S
	1	2	3	4	5	6
7	8	9	10	11	12	13
14	15	16	17	18	19	20
21	22	23	24	25	26	27
28						

I Long for ...

_____
_____
_____
_____
_____

Friday 21 January

8 am
_____

10 am
_____

12 pm
_____

2 pm
_____

4 pm
_____

6 pm
_____

December 2010

M	T	W	T	F	S	S
		1	2	3	4	5
6	7	8	9	10	11	12
13	14	15	16	17	18	19
20	21	22	23	24	25	26
27	28	29	30	31		

Today I am Grateful for . . .

Saturday 22 January

Sunday 23 January

Today I am Grateful for . . .

_____

_____

_____

_____

_____

Monday 24 January

8 am

_____

10 am

_____

12 pm

_____

2 pm

_____

4 pm

_____

6 pm

_____

Developing a burning desire to love and seek God is difficult when we have so many emotions within us that cause us to feel already rejected by him.

AJ Miller

December 2010						
M	T	W	T	F	S	S
		1	2	3	4	5
6	7	8	9	10	11	12
13	14	15	16	17	18	19
20	21	22	23	24	25	26
27	28	29	30	31		

Do I have a burning Desire to know God?

_____

_____

_____

_____

_____

_____

_____

Tuesday 25 January

8 am

_____

_____

10 am

_____

_____

12 pm

_____

_____

2 pm

_____

_____

4 pm

_____

_____

6 pm

_____

_____

| February 2011 | | | | | | |
M	T	W	T	F	S	S
	1	2	3	4	5	6
7	8	9	10	11	12	13
14	15	16	17	18	19	20
21	22	23	24	25	26	27
28						

Today I am Grateful for . . .

_____

_____

_____

_____

_____

_____

Third Quarter Waning Moon in Scorpio
*Temper the desire to push forward with the guidance of your
inner wisdom—listen to your gut instincts.*

Wednesday 26 January

8 am

10 am

12 pm

2 pm

4 pm

6 pm

	M	T	W	T	F	S	S
December 2010		1	2	3	4	5
	6	7	8	9	10	11	12
	13	14	15	16	17	18	19
	20	21	22	23	24	25	26
	27	28	29	30	31		

Today I am Grateful for . . .

_____
_____
_____
_____
_____
_____
_____

Thursday 27 January

8 am
_____
_____

10 am
_____
_____

12 pm
_____
_____

2 pm
_____
_____

4 pm
_____
_____

6 pm
_____
_____

February 2011

M	T	W	T	F	S	S
	1	2	3	4	5	6
7	8	9	10	11	12	13
14	15	16	17	18	19	20
21	22	23	24	25	26	27
28						

Today I am Grateful for . . .

_____
_____
_____
_____
_____
_____

Friday 28 January

8 am
_____
_____

10 am
_____
_____

12 pm
_____
_____

2 pm
_____
_____

4 pm
_____
_____

6 pm
_____
_____

			December 2010			
M	T	W	T	F	S	S
		1	2	3	4	5
6	7	8	9	10	11	12
13	14	15	16	17	18	19
20	21	22	23	24	25	26
27	28	29	30	31		

Today my Desires ...

Saturday 29 January

Sunday 30 January

Today I am Grateful for . . .

_____

_____

_____

_____

_____

Monday 31 January

8 am

10 am

12 pm

2 pm

4 pm

6 pm

A person can believe in their mind that they have a
passionate desire for something, but if that desire is
of the mind only and does not originate within the
soul, the thing longed for will not result at all.

AJ Miller

December 2010

M	T	W	T	F	S	S
		1	2	3	4	5
6	7	8	9	10	11	12
13	14	15	16	17	18	19
20	21	22	23	24	25	26
27	28	29	30	31		

Reflections on the Month

Attraction

Everything on earth
and in the spiritual world
is created through
the Law of Attraction.

Everything around you
is your Law of Attraction.

You created it.

AJ Miller

February

Photo by Marsel van Oosten

February 2011

Monday	Tuesday	Wednesday	Thursday	Friday	Saturday	Sunday
	1	2	3	4	5	6
7	8	9	10	11	12	13
14	15	16	17	18	19	20
21	22	23	24	25	26	27
28						

Today I Attracted ...

_____

_____

_____

_____

_____

_____

_____

Tuesday 1 February

8 am

10 am

12 pm

2 pm

4 pm

6 pm

		March 2011				
M	T	W	T	F	S	S
	1	2	3	4	5	6
7	8	9	10	11	12	13
14	15	16	17	18	19	20
21	22	23	24	25	26	27
28	29	30	31			

Today I am Grateful for . . .

_____

_____

_____

_____

_____

_____

Wednesday 2 February

8 am

_____

10 am

_____

12 pm

_____

2 pm

_____

4 pm

_____

6 pm

_____

_____

January 2011

M	T	W	T	F	S	S
					1	2
3	4	5	6	7	8	9
10	11	12	13	14	15	16
17	18	19	20	21	22	23
24	25	26	27	28	29	30
31						

Today I am Grateful for ...

○

_____

_____

_____

_____

_____

_____

_____

Thursday 3 February

New or Dark Moon in Aquarius
Idealism, determination and trust underpin the journey of this new moon. Multi-tasking and delegating will get the job done. Remember to nurture yourself and others along the way.

8 am

10 am

12 pm

2 pm

4 pm

6 pm

		March 2011				
M	T	W	T	F	S	S
	1	2	3	4	5	6
7	8	9	10	11	12	13
14	15	16	17	18	19	20
21	22	23	24	25	26	27
28	29	30	31			

Today I Created . . .

_____
_____
_____
_____
_____

Friday 4 February

8 am
_____
_____

10 am
_____
_____

12 pm
_____
_____

2 pm
_____
_____

4 pm
_____
_____

6 pm
_____
_____

January 2011

M	T	W	T	F	S	S
					1	2
3	4	5	6	7	8	9
10	11	12	13	14	15	16
17	18	19	20	21	22	23
24	25	26	27	28	29	30
31						

Today I am Grateful for . . .

Saturday 5 February

Sunday 6 February

Today I am Grateful for . . .

_____
_____
_____
_____
_____
_____

Monday 7 February

8 am
_____
_____

10 am
_____
_____

12 pm
_____
_____

2 pm
_____
_____

4 pm
_____
_____

6 pm
_____
_____

The purpose of the Law of Attraction is to help you release from your soul all of the emotions that are disharmonious with love, and to allow emotions which are harmonious with love to enter you.

AJ Miller

January 2011

M	T	W	T	F	S	S
					1	2
3	4	5	6	7	8	9
10	11	12	13	14	15	16
17	18	19	20	21	22	23
24	25	26	27	28	29	30
31						

Today I am Grateful for . . .

_____

_____

_____

_____

_____

_____

Tuesday 8 February

8 am

_____

_____

10 am

_____

_____

12 pm

_____

_____

2 pm

_____

_____

4 pm

_____

_____

6 pm

_____

_____

March 2011

M	T	W	T	F	S	S
	1	2	3	4	5	6
7	8	9	10	11	12	13
14	15	16	17	18	19	20
21	22	23	24	25	26	27
28	29	30	31			

Today I am Grateful for . . .

_____
_____
_____
_____
_____
_____

Wednesday 9 February

8 am
_____
_____

10 am
_____
_____

12 pm
_____
_____

2 pm
_____
_____

4 pm
_____
_____

6 pm
_____
_____

January 2011						
M	T	W	T	F	S	S
					1	2
3	4	5	6	7	8	9
10	11	12	13	14	15	16
17	18	19	20	21	22	23
24	25	26	27	28	29	30
31						

I take Responsibility for . . .

_____

_____

_____

_____

_____

_____

Thursday 10 February

8 am

_____

_____

10 am

_____

_____

12 pm

_____

_____

2 pm

_____

_____

4 pm

_____

_____

6 pm

_____

_____

March 2011						
M	T	W	T	F	S	S
	1	2	3	4	5	6
7	8	9	10	11	12	13
14	15	16	17	18	19	20
21	22	23	24	25	26	27
28	29	30	31			

Today I am Grateful for . . .

_____
_____
_____
_____
_____
_____

First Quarter Waxing Moon in Taurus
*Abundance and wellbeing is based partly on your mindset so listen
to your own sense of knowing your path from deep within.*

Friday 11 February

8 am

10 am

12 pm

2 pm

4 pm

6 pm

		January 2011				
M	T	W	T	F	S	S
					1	2
3	4	5	6	7	8	9
10	11	12	13	14	15	16
17	18	19	20	21	22	23
24	25	26	27	28	29	30
31						

Today I am Grateful for . . .

Saturday 12 February

Sunday 13 February

Today I am Grateful for . . .

Monday 14 February

8 am

---

10 am

---

12 pm

---

2 pm

---

4 pm

---

6 pm

A lover represents the love you feel for your parents, your children, your brothers, your sisters, your friends, your enemies. That's why they are so attractive. They sum up in one person all of the beings in your life.

Ramtha

			January 2011			
M	T	W	T	F	S	S
					1	2
3	4	5	6	7	8	9
10	11	12	13	14	15	16
17	18	19	20	21	22	23
24	25	26	27	28	29	30
31						

Today I am Grateful for . . .

_____

_____

_____

_____

_____

_____

Tuesday 15 February

8 am

_____

_____

10 am

_____

_____

12 pm

_____

_____

2 pm

_____

_____

4 pm

_____

_____

6 pm

_____

_____

March 2011

M	T	W	T	F	S	S
	1	2	3	4	5	6
7	8	9	10	11	12	13
14	15	16	17	18	19	20
21	22	23	24	25	26	27
28	29	30	31			

I am Responsible for ...

_____

_____

_____

_____

_____

Wednesday 16 February

8 am

10 am

12 pm

2 pm

4 pm

6 pm

January 2011

M	T	W	T	F	S	S
					1	2
3	4	5	6	7	8	9
10	11	12	13	14	15	16
17	18	19	20	21	22	23
24	25	26	27	28	29	30
31						

Today I am Grateful for . . .

_____

_____

_____

_____

_____

_____

_____

Thursday 17 February

8 am

_____

_____

10 am

_____

_____

12 pm

_____

_____

2 pm

_____

_____

4 pm

_____

_____

6 pm

_____

_____

			March 2011			
M	T	W	T	F	S	S
	1	2	3	4	5	6
7	8	9	10	11	12	13
14	15	16	17	18	19	20
21	22	23	24	25	26	27
28	29	30	31			

Today I am Grateful for . . .

_____

_____

_____

_____

_____

_____

Full Moon in Leo
Sometimes we are what we do so pause for a moment and reflect upon what you do with your time and where you want your life to be focused. It is a good time to discuss your ideas with others.

Friday 18 February

8 am

10 am

12 pm

2 pm

4 pm

6 pm

	January 2011					
M	T	W	T	F	S	S
					1	2
3	4	5	6	7	8	9
10	11	12	13	14	15	16
17	18	19	20	21	22	23
24	25	26	27	28	29	30
31						

Today I am Grateful for . . .

Saturday 19 February

Sunday 20 February

Today I am Grateful for . . .

_____
_____
_____
_____
_____

Monday 21 February

8 am
_____
_____

10 am
_____
_____

12 pm
_____
_____

2 pm
_____
_____

4 pm
_____
_____

6 pm
_____
_____

If your Law of Attraction is bringing to you negative emotions or situations, we must firstly deal with the judgments we put upon ourselves about it.

AJ Miller

January 2011

M	T	W	T	F	S	S
					1	2
3	4	5	6	7	8	9
10	11	12	13	14	15	16
17	18	19	20	21	22	23
24	25	26	27	28	29	30
31						

I take Ownership of . . .

Tuesday 22 February

8 am

10 am

12 pm

2 pm

4 pm

6 pm

Today I am Grateful for . . .

_____

_____

_____

_____

_____

Wednesday 23 February

8 am

_____

10 am

_____

12 pm

_____

2 pm

_____

4 pm

_____

6 pm

_____

		January 2011				
M	T	W	T	F	S	S
					1	2
3	4	5	6	7	8	9
10	11	12	13	14	15	16
17	18	19	20	21	22	23
24	25	26	27	28	29	30
31						

Today I Attracted . . .

_____

_____

_____

_____

_____

_____

_____

Thursday 24 February

8 am
_____

_____

10 am
_____

_____

12 pm
_____

_____

2 pm
_____

_____

4 pm
_____

_____

6 pm
_____

_____

			March 2011			
M	T	W	T	F	S	S
	1	2	3	4	5	6
7	8	9	10	11	12	13
14	15	16	17	18	19	20
21	22	23	24	25	26	27
28	29	30	31			

Today I am Grateful for . . .

Third Quarter Waning Moon in Sagittarius
Excitement is in the air with a feeling that anything is possible.
Dream big!

Friday 25 February

8 am

10 am

12 pm

2 pm

4 pm

6 pm

	January 2011					
M	T	W	T	F	S	S
					1	2
3	4	5	6	7	8	9
10	11	12	13	14	15	16
17	18	19	20	21	22	23
24	25	26	27	28	29	30
31						

Today I am Grateful for . . .

Saturday 26 February

Sunday 27 February

I will no longer Judge myself for . . .

_____

_____

_____

_____

_____

Monday 28 February

8 am
_____

_____

10 am
_____

_____

12 pm
_____

_____

2 pm
_____

_____

4 pm
_____

_____

6 pm
_____

_____

Most of the time we do not trust our Law of Attraction. We walk away from what is being presented. We resist seeing ourselves.

AJ Miller

		January 2011				
M	T	W	T	F	S	S
					1	2
3	4	5	6	7	8	9
10	11	12	13	14	15	16
17	18	19	20	21	22	23
24	25	26	27	28	29	30
31						

Reflections on the Month

Romance

March

Those we have loved never leave us. They live on forever in our hearts, and cast their radiant light onto our every shadow.

Sylvana Rossetti

March 2011

Monday	Tuesday	Wednesday	Thursday	Friday	Saturday	Sunday
	1	2	3	4	5	6
7	8	9	10	11	12	13
14	15	16	17	18	19	20
21	22	23	24	25	26	27
28	29	30	31			

Today I am Grateful for . . .

_____

_____

_____

_____

_____

_____

Tuesday 1 March

8 am

_____

_____

10 am

_____

_____

12 pm

_____

_____

2 pm

_____

_____

4 pm

_____

_____

6 pm

_____

_____

		April 2011				
M	T	W	T	F	S	S
				1	2	3
4	5	6	7	8	9	10
11	12	13	14	15	16	17
18	19	20	21	22	23	24
25	26	27	28	29	30	

Today I am Grateful for . . .

_____

_____

_____

_____

_____

_____

Wednesday 2 March

8 am

_____

10 am

_____

12 pm

_____

2 pm

_____

4 pm

_____

6 pm

_____

February 2011						
M	T	W	T	F	S	S
	1	2	3	4	5	6
7	8	9	10	11	12	13
14	15	16	17	18	19	20
21	22	23	24	25	26	27
28						

Today I am Grateful for . . .

_____
_____
_____
_____
_____
_____
_____

Thursday 3 March

8 am
_____
_____

10 am
_____
_____

12 pm
_____
_____

2 pm
_____
_____

4 pm
_____
_____

6 pm
_____
_____

April 2011

M	T	W	T	F	S	S
				1	2	3
4	5	6	7	8	9	10
11	12	13	14	15	16	17
18	19	20	21	22	23	24
25	26	27	28	29	30	

Today I am Grateful for . . .

_____

_____

_____

_____

_____

_____

Friday 4 March

8 am
_____

_____

10 am
_____

_____

12 pm
_____

_____

2 pm
_____

_____

4 pm
_____

_____

6 pm
_____

_____

		February 2011				
M	T	W	T	F	S	S
	1	2	3	4	5	6
7	8	9	10	11	12	13
14	15	16	17	18	19	20
21	22	23	24	25	26	27
28						

Today I am Grateful for . . .

$\bigcirc$

New or Dark Moon in Pisces
When your desires align with your inner wellbeing, synchronicity and timing abound. Slip into the flow of life and let your rational mind enjoy the ride.

Saturday 5 March

Sunday 6 March

Today I am Grateful for . . .

_____

_____

_____

_____

_____

_____

Monday 7 March

8 am

10 am

12 pm

2 pm

4 pm

6 pm

To find someone who will love you for no reason, and to shower that person with reasons, that is the ultimate happiness.

Robert Brault

February 2011

M	T	W	T	F	S	S
	1	2	3	4	5	6
7	8	9	10	11	12	13
14	15	16	17	18	19	20
21	22	23	24	25	26	27
28						

Today I am Grateful for . . .

_____

_____

_____

_____

_____

_____

_____

Tuesday 8 March

8 am

10 am

12 pm

2 pm

4 pm

6 pm

April 2011

M	T	W	T	F	S	S
				1	2	3
4	5	6	7	8	9	10
11	12	13	14	15	16	17
18	19	20	21	22	23	24
25	26	27	28	29	30	

Today I am Grateful for . . .

Wednesday 9 March

8 am

10 am

12 pm

2 pm

4 pm

6 pm

February 2011

M	T	W	T	F	S	S
	1	2	3	4	5	6
7	8	9	10	11	12	13
14	15	16	17	18	19	20
21	22	23	24	25	26	27
28						

Today I am Grateful for . . .

_____

_____

_____

_____

_____

_____

_____

Thursday 10 March

8 am

_____

_____

10 am

_____

_____

12 pm

_____

_____

2 pm

_____

_____

4 pm

_____

_____

6 pm

_____

_____

April 2011

M	T	W	T	F	S	S
				1	2	3
4	5	6	7	8	9	10
11	12	13	14	15	16	17
18	19	20	21	22	23	24
25	26	27	28	29	30	

Today I am Grateful for . . .

Friday 11 March

8 am

10 am

12 pm

2 pm

4 pm

6 pm

		February 2011				
M	T	W	T	F	S	S
	1	2	3	4	5	6
7	8	9	10	11	12	13
14	15	16	17	18	19	20
21	22	23	24	25	26	27
28						

Today I am Grateful for . . .

_____

_____

_____

_____

_____

_____

_____

Saturday 12 March

_____

_____

_____

_____

_____

_____

_____

_____

First Quarter Waxing Moon in Gemini
With an abundance of inventive new ideas and solutions,
this is a great time for creative thinking and brainstorming.

Sunday 13 March

_____

_____

_____

_____

_____

_____

_____

_____

_____

Today I am Grateful for ...

_____

_____

_____

_____

_____

Monday 14 March

8 am

10 am

12 pm

2 pm

4 pm

6 pm

Girls we love for what they are: young men for what they promise to be.

Johann Wolfgang von Goethe

| | February 2011 | | | | | |
M	T	W	T	F	S	S
	1	2	3	4	5	6
7	8	9	10	11	12	13
14	15	16	17	18	19	20
21	22	23	24	25	26	27
28						

Today I am Grateful for . . .

_____

_____

_____

_____

_____

_____

Tuesday 15 March

8 am

_____

_____

10 am

_____

_____

12 pm

_____

_____

2 pm

_____

_____

4 pm

_____

_____

6 pm

_____

_____

April 2011						
M	T	W	T	F	S	S
				1	2	3
4	5	6	7	8	9	10
11	12	13	14	15	16	17
18	19	20	21	22	23	24
25	26	27	28	29	30	

Today I am Grateful for . . .

_____

_____

_____

_____

_____

_____

Wednesday 16 March

8 am

10 am

12 pm

2 pm

4 pm

6 pm

February 2011						
M	T	W	T	F	S	S
	1	2	3	4	5	6
7	8	9	10	11	12	13
14	15	16	17	18	19	20
21	22	23	24	25	26	27
28						

Today I am Grateful for . . .

_____
_____
_____
_____
_____
_____
_____

Thursday 17 March

8 am
_____
_____

10 am
_____
_____

12 pm
_____
_____

2 pm
_____
_____

4 pm
_____
_____

6 pm
_____
_____

April 2011						
M	T	W	T	F	S	S
				1	2	3
4	5	6	7	8	9	10
11	12	13	14	15	16	17
18	19	20	21	22	23	24
25	26	27	28	29	30	

Today I am Grateful for . . .

_____

_____

_____

_____

_____

_____

Friday 18 March

8 am

10 am

12 pm

2 pm

4 pm

6 pm

February 2011

M	T	W	T	F	S	S
	1	2	3	4	5	6
7	8	9	10	11	12	13
14	15	16	17	18	19	20
21	22	23	24	25	26	27
28						

Today I am Grateful for . . .

Saturday 19 March

Full Moon in Virgo
Patiently grounding and applying solutions to the practicalities of life, dare to be your own unique self.

Sunday 20 March

Today I am Grateful for ...

_____

_____

_____

_____

_____

_____

Monday 21 March

March Equinox

As the balance of day and night becomes equal, it is time to be thoughtful about the next step. Inspiration and inventiveness are in the air, so be sure that individual passions are in alignment with your long-term plans and goals. Collective ideology is changing and must be incorporated. If you resist too much there is quite a struggle as your old belief systems are challenged.

8 am

10 am

12 pm

2 pm

4 pm

6 pm

How on earth are you ever going to explain in terms of chemistry and physics so important a biological phenomenon as first love?

Albert Einstein

		February 2011				
M	T	W	T	F	S	S
	1	2	3	4	5	6
7	8	9	10	11	12	13
14	15	16	17	18	19	20
21	22	23	24	25	26	27
28						

Today I am Grateful for . . .

_____
_____
_____
_____
_____
_____
_____

Tuesday 22 March

8 am
_____
_____

10 am
_____
_____

12 pm
_____
_____

2 pm
_____
_____

4 pm
_____
_____

6 pm
_____
_____

| April 2011 | | | | | | |
M	T	W	T	F	S	S
				1	2	3
4	5	6	7	8	9	10
11	12	13	14	15	16	17
18	19	20	21	22	23	24
25	26	27	28	29	30	

Today I am Grateful for . . .

Wednesday 23 March

8 am

10 am

12 pm

2 pm

4 pm

6 pm

February 2011

M	T	W	T	F	S	S
	1	2	3	4	5	6
7	8	9	10	11	12	13
14	15	16	17	18	19	20
21	22	23	24	25	26	27
28						

Today I am Grateful for ...

_____

_____

_____

_____

_____

_____

Thursday 24 March

8 am

_____

_____

10 am

_____

_____

12 pm

_____

_____

2 pm

_____

_____

4 pm

_____

_____

6 pm

_____

_____

_____

| April 2011 | | | | | | |
M	T	W	T	F	S	S
				1	2	3
4	5	6	7	8	9	10
11	12	13	14	15	16	17
18	19	20	21	22	23	24
25	26	27	28	29	30	

Today I am Grateful for . . .

_____

_____

_____

_____

_____

_____

Friday 25 March

8 am

_____

10 am

_____

12 pm

_____

2 pm

_____

4 pm

_____

6 pm

_____

		February 2011				
M	T	W	T	F	S	S
	1	2	3	4	5	6
7	8	9	10	11	12	13
14	15	16	17	18	19	20
21	22	23	24	25	26	27
28						

Today I am Grateful for . . .

Saturday 26 March

Third Quarter Waning Moon in Capricorn
A collective pause before you hit the power button. Are your plans well thought out? Have you been preparing for future changes?

Sunday 27 March

Today I am Grateful for ...

_____
_____
_____
_____
_____
_____

Monday 28 March

8 am
_____

10 am
_____

12 pm
_____

2 pm
_____

4 pm
_____

6 pm
_____

Being loved by all is little fun unless you're also loved by one.

Robert Brault

		February 2011				
M	T	W	T	F	S	S
	1	2	3	4	5	6
7	8	9	10	11	12	13
14	15	16	17	18	19	20
21	22	23	24	25	26	27
28						

Today I am Grateful for . . .

_____

_____

_____

_____

_____

_____

_____

Tuesday 29 March

8 am
_____

_____

10 am
_____

_____

12 pm
_____

_____

2 pm
_____

_____

4 pm
_____

_____

6 pm
_____

_____

		April 2011				
M	T	W	T	F	S	S
				1	2	3
4	5	6	7	8	9	10
11	12	13	14	15	16	17
18	19	20	21	22	23	24
25	26	27	28	29	30	

Today I am Grateful for . . .

_____

_____

_____

_____

_____

Wednesday 30 March

8 am

_____

10 am

_____

12 pm

_____

2 pm

_____

4 pm

_____

6 pm

_____

February 2011

M	T	W	T	F	S	S
	1	2	3	4	5	6
7	8	9	10	11	12	13
14	15	16	17	18	19	20
21	22	23	24	25	26	27
28						

Today I am Grateful for ...

_____

_____

_____

_____

_____

_____

_____

_____

_____

Thursday 31 March

8 am

_____

_____

10 am

_____

_____

12 pm

_____

_____

2 pm

_____

_____

4 pm

_____

_____

6 pm

_____

_____

April 2011						
M	T	W	T	F	S	S
				1	2	3
4	5	6	7	8	9	10
11	12	13	14	15	16	17
18	19	20	21	22	23	24
25	26	27	28	29	30	

Reflections on the Month

Make us worthy, Lord, to serve our fellow men
throughout the world
Who live and die in poverty and hunger.

Give them, through our hands, this day, their
daily bread,
And by our understanding love give peace and joy.

Lord, make men a channel of Thy peace.
That where there is hatred I may bring love,
That where there is wrong I may bring the spirit
of forgiveness;
That where there is discord I may bring harmony,
That where there is error, I may bring truth,
That where there is doubt, I may bring faith,
That where there is despair, I may bring hope,
That where there are shadows, I may bring light,
That where there is sadness, I may bring joy.
Lord, grant that I may seek rather to comfort,
than to be comforted,
To understand than to be understood,
To love than to be loved,
For it is by forgetting self that one finds,
It is by forgiving that one is forgiven,
It is by dying that one awakens to eternal life.

Amen

A Prayer by Mother Teresa

Projection

Projection occurs when there has first been denial within yourself.

Projection is an act in which you psychically try to throw out of your ownership everything that you have judged as being despicable or unworthy of you, something you don't want. And so you will project it. You will throw it up and out, and let it land on whoever happens to be nearby.

www.divinetruth.com.au

April

April 2011

Monday	Tuesday	Wednesday	Thursday	Friday	Saturday	Sunday
			1	2	3	
4	5	6	7	8	9	10
11	12	13	14	15	16	17
18	19	20	21	22	23	24
25	26	27	28	29	30	

Today I am Grateful for . . .

_____
_____
_____
_____
_____
_____

Friday 1 April

8 am
_____
_____

10 am
_____
_____

12 pm
_____
_____

2 pm
_____
_____

4 pm
_____
_____

6 pm
_____
_____

| May 2011 | | | | | | |
M	T	W	T	F	S	S
						1
2	3	4	5	6	7	8
9	10	11	12	13	14	15
16	17	18	19	20	21	22
23	24	25	26	27	28	29
30	31					

How have I Judged another Today . . .

Saturday 2 April

Sunday 3 April

Today I am Grateful for . . .

○

_____

_____

_____

_____

_____

_____

_____

Monday 4 April

New or Dark Moon in Aries

An adventurous New Moon. Being able to step outside the boundaries of the established order is a good thing. Let your choices be driven by what you consider gives you quality rather than quantity. Listen to your intuition.

8 am

10 am

12 pm

2 pm

4 pm

6 pm

Each time that you judge anything or anyone, you have literally elicited guilt within _yourself_ because there is a place within you, yet still, that knows the perfect purity of your brother and sister, and sees quite clearly that all things within the human realm are either the extension of Love, or a cry for help and healing.

www.divinetruth.com.au

May 2011

M	T	W	T	F	S	S
						1
2	3	4	5	6	7	8
9	10	11	12	13	14	15
16	17	18	19	20	21	22
23	24	25	26	27	28	29
30	31					

Today I am Grateful for . . .

Tuesday 5 April

8 am

10 am

12 pm

2 pm

4 pm

6 pm

		March 2011				
M	T	W	T	F	S	S
	1	2	3	4	5	6
7	8	9	10	11	12	13
14	15	16	17	18	19	20
21	22	23	24	25	26	27
28	29	30	31			

How have I Judged myself Today . . .

_____

_____

_____

_____

_____

_____

Wednesday 6 April

8 am
_____

_____

10 am
_____

_____

12 pm
_____

_____

2 pm
_____

_____

4 pm
_____

_____

6 pm
_____

_____

_____

			May 2011			
M	T	W	T	F	S	S
						1
2	3	4	5	6	7	8
9	10	11	12	13	14	15
16	17	18	19	20	21	22
23	24	25	26	27	28	29
30	31					

Today I am Grateful for . . .

_____

_____

_____

_____

_____

Thursday 7 April

8 am
_____

_____

10 am
_____

_____

12 pm
_____

_____

2 pm
_____

_____

4 pm
_____

_____

6 pm
_____

_____

| | | | March 2011 | | | |
M	T	W	T	F	S	S
	1	2	3	4	5	6
7	8	9	10	11	12	13
14	15	16	17	18	19	20
21	22	23	24	25	26	27
28	29	30	31			

How am I Judging others?

_____

_____

_____

_____

_____

_____

Friday 8 April

8 am

_____

10 am

_____

12 pm

_____

2 pm

_____

4 pm

_____

6 pm

_____

			May 2011			
M	T	W	T	F	S	S
						1
2	3	4	5	6	7	8
9	10	11	12	13	14	15
16	17	18	19	20	21	22
23	24	25	26	27	28	29
30	31					

Am I Seeing myself in a negative light . . .

Saturday 9 April

Sunday 10 April

Today I am Grateful for . . .

_____

_____

_____

_____

_____

_____

Monday 11 April

First Quarter Waxing Moon in Cancer
Are you truly standing and listening to your inner truths? If so, great opportunities await; if not, then reconsider what your priorities are in life. Take a moment to restore and balance your passionate self.

8 am

10 am

12 pm

2 pm

4 pm

6 pm

Projection is the denial of the Truth that nothing you experience has been caused by anything outside of you. The attempt to *insist* that reality is other than the way God made it. That you are not powerful, that you are a victim of circumstance, that you're in a world that can actually do things to you and make you... cause you to make decisions that you wouldn't have made otherwise. That is always denial. And it is a lie.

www.divinetruth.com.au

			May 2011			
M	T	W	T	F	S	S
						1
2	3	4	5	6	7	8
9	10	11	12	13	14	15
16	17	18	19	20	21	22
23	24	25	26	27	28	29
30	31					

Today I am Grateful for . . .

_____
_____
_____
_____
_____
_____

Tuesday 12 April

8 am

10 am

12 pm

2 pm

4 pm

6 pm

	March 2011					
M	T	W	T	F	S	S
	1	2	3	4	5	6
7	8	9	10	11	12	13
14	15	16	17	18	19	20
21	22	23	24	25	26	27
28	29	30	31			

Today I am Grateful for . . .

_____
_____
_____
_____
_____
_____

Wednesday 13 April

8 am

10 am

12 pm

2 pm

4 pm

6 pm

		May 2011				
M	T	W	T	F	S	S
						1
2	3	4	5	6	7	8
9	10	11	12	13	14	15
16	17	18	19	20	21	22
23	24	25	26	27	28	29
30	31					

Today I am Grateful for . . .

_____

_____

_____

_____

_____

Thursday 14 April

8 am

_____

10 am

_____

12 pm

_____

2 pm

_____

4 pm

_____

6 pm

_____

		March 2011				
M	T	W	T	F	S	S
	1	2	3	4	5	6
7	8	9	10	11	12	13
14	15	16	17	18	19	20
21	22	23	24	25	26	27
28	29	30	31			

How am I Judging myself?

_____
_____
_____
_____
_____
_____
_____

Friday 15 April

8 am
_____
_____

10 am
_____
_____

12 pm
_____
_____

2 pm
_____
_____

4 pm
_____
_____

6 pm
_____
_____

		May 2011				
M	T	W	T	F	S	S
						1
2	3	4	5	6	7	8
9	10	11	12	13	14	15
16	17	18	19	20	21	22
23	24	25	26	27	28	29
30	31					

What Emotions do I avoid Feeling?

Saturday 16 April

Sunday 17 April

Today I am Grateful for . . .

_____
_____
_____
_____
_____
_____

Full Moon in Libra
Follow your bliss towards a better life. Practice responding in a positive manner. What drives the restlessness to get things done? What lights your fire?

Monday 18 April

8 am
_____
_____

10 am
_____
_____

12 pm
_____
_____

2 pm
_____
_____

4 pm
_____
_____

6 pm
_____
_____

The shadow is the easiest of the archetypes for most persons to experience. We tend to see it in "others". That is to say, we project our dark side onto others and thus interpret them as "enemies" or as "exotic" presences that fascinate.

www.divinetruth.com.au

May 2011

M	T	W	T	F	S	S
						1
2	3	4	5	6	7	8
9	10	11	12	13	14	15
16	17	18	19	20	21	22
23	24	25	26	27	28	29
30	31					

Today I am Grateful for . . .

Tuesday 19 April

8 am

10 am

12 pm

2 pm

4 pm

6 pm

March 2011

M	T	W	T	F	S	S
	1	2	3	4	5	6
7	8	9	10	11	12	13
14	15	16	17	18	19	20
21	22	23	24	25	26	27
28	29	30	31			

Am I Projecting my emotions . . .

_____
_____
_____
_____
_____
_____

Wednesday 20 April

8 am
_____
_____

10 am
_____
_____

12 pm
_____
_____

2 pm
_____
_____

4 pm
_____
_____

6 pm
_____
_____

May 2011						
M	T	W	T	F	S	S
						1
2	3	4	5	6	7	8
9	10	11	12	13	14	15
16	17	18	19	20	21	22
23	24	25	26	27	28	29
30	31					

What Emotions do I avoid Feeling?

_____

_____

_____

_____

_____

_____

Thursday 21 April

8 am
_____

_____

10 am
_____

_____

12 pm
_____

_____

2 pm
_____

_____

4 pm
_____

_____

6 pm
_____

_____

		March 2011				
M	T	W	T	F	S	S
	1	2	3	4	5	6
7	8	9	10	11	12	13
14	15	16	17	18	19	20
21	22	23	24	25	26	27
28	29	30	31			

Today I am Grateful for . . .

_____
_____
_____
_____
_____
_____

Friday 22 April

8 am
_____
_____

10 am
_____
_____

12 pm
_____
_____

2 pm
_____
_____

4 pm
_____
_____

6 pm
_____
_____

			May 2011			
M	T	W	T	F	S	S
						1
2	3	4	5	6	7	8
9	10	11	12	13	14	15
16	17	18	19	20	21	22
23	24	25	26	27	28	29
30	31					

Today I am Grateful for . . .

Saturday 23 April

Sunday 24 April

Today I am Grateful for . . .

_____
_____
_____
_____
_____
_____
_____

Third Quarter Waning Moon in Aquarius
Oh my gosh! The green lights come on and delays or confusions clear up.
Hold on because it's quite a ride this week.

Monday 25 April

8 am
_____

10 am
_____

12 pm
_____

2 pm
_____

4 pm
_____

6 pm
_____

Hell is oneself, Hell is alone, the other figures in it merely projections.

TS Eliot

May 2011

M	T	W	T	F	S	S
						1
2	3	4	5	6	7	8
9	10	11	12	13	14	15
16	17	18	19	20	21	22
23	24	25	26	27	28	29
30	31					

Today I am Grateful for . . .

_____
_____
_____
_____
_____
_____

Tuesday 26 April

8 am
_____
_____

10 am
_____
_____

12 pm
_____
_____

2 pm
_____
_____

4 pm
_____
_____

6 pm
_____
_____

		March 2011				
M	T	W	T	F	S	S
	1	2	3	4	5	6
7	8	9	10	11	12	13
14	15	16	17	18	19	20
21	22	23	24	25	26	27
28	29	30	31			

How have I Judged another Today . . .

_____
_____
_____
_____
_____
_____

Wednesday 27 April

8 am
_____

_____

10 am
_____

_____

12 pm
_____

_____

2 pm
_____

_____

4 pm
_____

_____

6 pm
_____

_____

		May 2011				
M	T	W	T	F	S	S
						1
2	3	4	5	6	7	8
9	10	11	12	13	14	15
16	17	18	19	20	21	22
23	24	25	26	27	28	29
30	31					

Today I am Grateful for . . .

_____

_____

_____

_____

_____

Thursday 28 April

8 am

10 am

12 pm

2 pm

4 pm

6 pm

March 2011

M	T	W	T	F	S	S
	1	2	3	4	5	6
7	8	9	10	11	12	13
14	15	16	17	18	19	20
21	22	23	24	25	26	27
28	29	30	31			

What Emotions do I avoid Feeling?

_____
_____
_____
_____
_____
_____

Friday 29 April

8 am
_____

_____

10 am
_____

_____

12 pm
_____

_____

2 pm
_____

_____

4 pm
_____

_____

6 pm
_____

_____

May 2011						
M	T	W	T	F	S	S
						1
2	3	4	5	6	7	8
9	10	11	12	13	14	15
16	17	18	19	20	21	22
23	24	25	26	27	28	29
30	31					

Today I am Grateful for . . .

Saturday 30 April

Why all this talk of the Beloved,

Music and dancing, and liquid ruby

Light we can lift in a cup?

Because it is low tide,

A very low tide in this age and around most hearts.

We are exquisite coral reefs,

Dying when exposed to strange elements.

God is the wine ocean we crave we miss

Flowing in and out of our pores.

Reflections on the Month

Addiction

May

Just sit there right now, don't do a thing. Just rest.
For your separation from God is the hardest work in this world.
Let me bring you trays of food and something that you like to drink.
You can use my soft words as a cushion for your head.

The Subject Tonight is Love, 60 Wild & Sweet Poems of Hafiz,
copyright 1996 and 2003 Daniel Ladinsky and used with his permission

May 2011

Monday	Tuesday	Wednesday	Thursday	Friday	Saturday	Sunday
						1
2	3	4	5	6	7	8
9	10	11	12	13	14	15
16	17	18	19	20	21	22
23	24	25	26	27	28	29
30	31					

Today I am Grateful for . . .

What are my addictions with my Partner?
Examples:
- I want them to listen to me—could indicate I have a wound about not being heard.
- I want them to find me sexy and desirable—I may already feel unattractive, insecure.
- I want my partner to take care of me—could indicate not feeling safe in the world.

Allow yourself to experience the underlying emotions that drive the addictions.

Sunday 1 May

Today I am Grateful for . . .

_____

_____

_____

_____

_____

_____

Monday 2 May

8 am

10 am

12 pm

2 pm

4 pm

6 pm

Sometimes a couple needs to step apart and make a space
between that each might see the other anew—in a glance
across a room or silhouetted against the moon.

Robert Brault

April 2011

M	T	W	T	F	S	S
				1	2	3
4	5	6	7	8	9	10
11	12	13	14	15	16	17
18	19	20	21	22	23	24
25	26	27	28	29	30	

Today I am Grateful for . . .

◯

Tuesday 3 May

New or Dark Moon in Taurus
Relationships with loved ones and children are about nourishing each other's souls. Do something together.

8 am

10 am

12 pm

2 pm

4 pm

6 pm

June 2011

M	T	W	T	F	S	S
		1	2	3	4	5
6	7	8	9	10	11	12
13	14	15	16	17	18	19
20	21	22	23	24	25	26
27	28	29	30			

Today I am Grateful for . . .

_____

_____

_____

_____

_____

Wednesday 4 May

8 am
_____

_____

10 am
_____

_____

12 pm
_____

_____

2 pm
_____

_____

4 pm
_____

_____

6 pm
_____

_____

_____

| | | | April 2011 | | | |
M	T	W	T	F	S	S
				1	2	3
4	5	6	7	8	9	10
11	12	13	14	15	16	17
18	19	20	21	22	23	24
25	26	27	28	29	30	

What am I Addicted to?

_____

_____

_____

_____

_____

_____

_____

Thursday 5 May

8 am

10 am

12 pm

2 pm

4 pm

6 pm

Addictions are habits that have power over us.
Habits become habits to comfort and help us.
But at what price comfort comes.
Wake up!
God has more to teach us.

Sara-Josephine

June 2011

M	T	W	T	F	S	S
		1	2	3	4	5
6	7	8	9	10	11	12
13	14	15	16	17	18	19
20	21	22	23	24	25	26
27	28	29	30			

Today I am Grateful for . . .

Friday 6 May

8 am

10 am

12 pm

2 pm

4 pm

6 pm

April 2011

M	T	W	T	F	S	
				1	2	3
4	5	6	7	8	9	
11	12	13	14	15	16	1
18	19	20	21	22	23	2
25	26	27	28	29	30	

Today I am Grateful for . . .

Saturday 7 May

Sunday 8 May

Today I am Grateful for . . .

_____

_____

_____

_____

_____

_____

Monday 9 May

8 am

_____

10 am

_____

12 pm

_____

2 pm

_____

4 pm

_____

6 pm

_____

All addictions are harmful whether physical, sexual, emotional or spiritual, and must be healed in order to receive divine love to the point of atonement.

AJ Miller

April 2011

M	T	W	T	F	S
				1	2
4	5	6	7	8	9
11	12	13	14	15	16
18	19	20	21	22	23
25	26	27	28	29	30

Today I am Grateful for . . .

_____

_____

_____

_____

_____

_____

_____

Tuesday 10 May

8 am

_____

_____

10 am

_____

_____

12 pm

_____

_____

2 pm

_____

_____

4 pm

_____

_____

6 pm

_____

_____

| | | June 2011 | | | | |
M	T	W	T	F	S	S
		1	2	3	4	5
6	7	8	9	10	11	12
13	14	15	16	17	18	19
20	21	22	23	24	25	26
27	28	29	30			

Today I am Grateful for . . .

Wednesday 11 May

First Quarter Waxing Moon in Leo
Very energetic and driven energy. The balance must be kept around work and health. Be pro-active.

8 am

10 am

12 pm

2 pm

4 pm

6 pm

April 2011

M	T	W	T	F	S	
				1	2	3
4	5	6	7	8	9	
11	12	13	14	15	16	
18	19	20	21	22	23	
25	26	27	28	29	30	

What can I not Live without?

_____

_____

_____

_____

_____

_____

_____

Thursday 12 May

8 am
_____

_____

10 am
_____

_____

12 pm
_____

_____

2 pm
_____

_____

4 pm
_____

_____

6 pm
_____

_____

June 2011

M	T	W	T	F	S	S
		1	2	3	4	5
6	7	8	9	10	11	12
13	14	15	16	17	18	19
20	21	22	23	24	25	26
27	28	29	30			

Today I am Grateful for ...

_____
_____
_____
_____
_____
_____

Friday 13 May

8 am
_____
_____

10 am
_____
_____

12 pm
_____
_____

2 pm
_____
_____

4 pm
_____
_____

6 pm
_____
_____

April 2011

M	T	W	T	F	S	
				1	2	
4	5	6	7	8	9	
11	12	13	14	15	16	
18	19	20	21	22	23	
25	26	27	28	29	30	

Today I am Grateful for . . .

_____
_____
_____
_____
_____
_____
_____
_____

Saturday 14 May

_____
_____
_____
_____
_____
_____
_____
_____
_____
_____

Sunday 15 May

_____
_____
_____
_____
_____
_____
_____
_____
_____
_____

Today I am Grateful for . . .

_____

_____

_____

_____

_____

_____

Monday 16 May

8 am

10 am

12 pm

2 pm

4 pm

6 pm

Addiction sidetracks and eclipses the energy of our deepest, truest desire for love and goodness. We succumb because the energy of our desire becomes attached to specific behaviours, objects, or people. Attachment is the process that enslaves desire and creates the state of addiction.

Gerald G May MD, Addiction and Grace

April 2011

M	T	W	T	F	S
				1	2
4	5	6	7	8	9
11	12	13	14	15	16
18	19	20	21	22	23
25	26	27	28	29	30

Today I am Grateful for ...

_____

_____

_____

_____

_____

_____

_____

Tuesday 17 May

Full Moon in Scorpio
Focus on who or what inspires you. Your wellbeing is really important.

8 am

_____

10 am

_____

12 pm

_____

2 pm

_____

4 pm

_____

6 pm

_____

		June 2011				
M	T	W	T	F	S	S
		1	2	3	4	5
6	7	8	9	10	11	12
13	14	15	16	17	18	19
20	21	22	23	24	25	26
27	28	29	30			

Where is my Focus today?

Wednesday 18 May

8 am

10 am

12 pm

2 pm

4 pm

6 pm

		April 2011			
M	T	W	T	F	S
				1	2
4	5	6	7	8	9
11	12	13	14	15	16
18	19	20	21	22	23
25	26	27	28	29	30

Today I am Grateful for . . .

Thursday 19 May

8 am

10 am

12 pm

2 pm

4 pm

6 pm

<table>
<tr><td colspan="7">June 2011</td></tr>
<tr><td>M</td><td>T</td><td>W</td><td>T</td><td>F</td><td>S</td><td>S</td></tr>
<tr><td></td><td></td><td>1</td><td>2</td><td>3</td><td>4</td><td>5</td></tr>
<tr><td>6</td><td>7</td><td>8</td><td>9</td><td>10</td><td>11</td><td>12</td></tr>
<tr><td>13</td><td>14</td><td>15</td><td>16</td><td>17</td><td>18</td><td>19</td></tr>
<tr><td>20</td><td>21</td><td>22</td><td>23</td><td>24</td><td>25</td><td>26</td></tr>
<tr><td>27</td><td>28</td><td>29</td><td>30</td><td></td><td></td><td></td></tr>
</table>

Today I am Grateful for . . .

_____
_____
_____
_____
_____
_____

Friday 20 May

8 am
_____
_____

10 am
_____
_____

12 pm
_____
_____

2 pm
_____
_____

4 pm
_____
_____

6 pm
_____
_____

April 2011

M	T	W	T	F	S	
				1	2	3
4	5	6	7	8	9	10
11	12	13	14	15	16	1
18	19	20	21	22	23	2
25	26	27	28	29	30	

Am I Doing what I Love?

Saturday 21 May

Sunday 22 May

Today I am Grateful for . . .

_____

_____

_____

_____

_____

Monday 23 May

8 am

10 am

12 pm

2 pm

4 pm

6 pm

I saw by the duck pond an elderly couple throwing crumbs on the water, close against each other, thinking each other's thoughts, casting each other's shadow, and I thought how little it mattered—which had been the great love and which the acquired taste that became an addiction.

Robert Brault

April 2011

M	T	W	T	F	S	
				1	2	3
4	5	6	7	8	9	1
11	12	13	14	15	16	1
18	19	20	21	22	23	2
25	26	27	28	29	30	

Today I am Grateful for . . .

_____
_____
_____
_____
_____
_____
_____

Tuesday 24 May

8 am
_____
_____

10 am
_____
_____

12 pm
_____
_____

2 pm
_____
_____

4 pm
_____
_____

6 pm
_____
_____

		June 2011				
M	T	W	T	F	S	S
		1	2	3	4	5
6	7	8	9	10	11	12
13	14	15	16	17	18	19
20	21	22	23	24	25	26
27	28	29	30			

Today I am Grateful for ...

_____

_____

_____

_____

_____

_____

Wednesday 25 May

Third Quarter Waning Moon in Pisces
Tasks abound and solutions flow. Approach decisions with integrity and planning, yet allow for random synchronicity.

8 am

10 am

12 pm

2 pm

4 pm

6 pm

April 2011

M	T	W	T	F	S	
				1	2	3
4	5	6	7	8	9	10
11	12	13	14	15	16	17
18	19	20	21	22	23	24
25	26	27	28	29	30	

Today I am Grateful for . . .

_____
_____
_____
_____
_____
_____

Thursday 26 May

8 am
_____
_____

10 am
_____
_____

12 pm
_____
_____

2 pm
_____
_____

4 pm
_____
_____

6 pm
_____
_____

		June 2011				
M	T	W	T	F	S	S
		1	2	3	4	5
6	7	8	9	10	11	12
13	14	15	16	17	18	19
20	21	22	23	24	25	26
27	28	29	30			

Today I am Grateful for . . .

_____

_____

_____

_____

_____

Friday 27 May

8 am

10 am

12 pm

2 pm

4 pm

6 pm

April 2011

M	T	W	T	F	S	
				1	2	3
4	5	6	7	8	9	1
11	12	13	14	15	16	1
18	19	20	21	22	23	2
25	26	27	28	29	30	

What am I Attached to?

Saturday 28 May

Sunday 29 May

Today I am Grateful for ...

_____
_____
_____
_____
_____
_____

Monday 30 May

8 am
_____

10 am
_____

12 pm
_____

2 pm
_____

4 pm
_____

6 pm
_____

Everyone is addicted to something. Drugs, alcohol, sex, work, food, love or romance. This is not the problem. The problem is the way we judge ourselves for having such attachments, making it impossible for any surrender to occur.

Melanie Spears

April 2011

M	T	W	T	F	S	
				1	2	3
4	5	6	7	8	9	
11	12	13	14	15	16	
18	19	20	21	22	23	
25	26	27	28	29	30	

Today I am Grateful for . . .

_____
_____
_____
_____
_____
_____
_____
_____

Tuesday 31 May

8 am
_____
_____
_____

10 am
_____
_____
_____

12 pm
_____
_____
_____

2 pm
_____
_____
_____

4 pm
_____
_____
_____

6 pm
_____
_____

June 2011

M	T	W	T	F	S	S
		1	2	3	4	5
6	7	8	9	10	11	12
13	14	15	16	17	18	19
20	21	22	23	24	25	26
27	28	29	30			

Reflections on the Month

Reflections on the Month

Separation

Don't surrender your loneliness
So quickly.
Let it cut more deep.

Let it ferment and season you
As few human
Or even divine ingredients can.

Something missing in my heart tonight
Has made my eyes so soft,
My voice so tender,
My need for God

Absolutely clear.

The Subject Tonight is Love, 60 Wild & Sweet Poems of Hafiz,
copyright 1996 and 2003 Daniel Ladinsky and used with his permission.

June

June 2011

Monday	Tuesday	Wednesday	Thursday	Friday	Saturday	Sunday
		1	2	3	4	5
6	7	8	9	10	11	12
13	14	15	16	17	18	19
20	21	22	23	24	25	26
27	28	29	30			

Today I am Grateful for . . .

_____
_____
_____
_____
_____
_____
_____

Wednesday 1 June

8 am
_____
_____

10 am
_____
_____

12 pm
_____
_____

2 pm
_____
_____

4 pm
_____
_____

6 pm
_____
_____

		July 2011				
M	T	W	T	F	S	S
				1	2	3
4	5	6	7	8	9	10
11	12	13	14	15	16	17
18	19	20	21	22	23	24
25	26	27	28	29	30	31

Today I am Grateful for ...

_____
_____
_____
_____
_____
_____

Thursday 2 June

New Moon in Gemini © **Solar Eclipse** (partial) in Gemini 11°Gem 01′
A truthful and gracious attitude towards communication is needed to expand
through the frustration that limits one's growth. Beware of undercurrents.

8 am

10 am

12 pm

2 pm

4 pm

6 pm

	May 2011					
M	T	W	T	F	S	S
						1
2	3	4	5	6	7	8
9	10	11	12	13	14	15
16	17	18	19	20	21	22
23	24	25	26	27	28	29
30	31					

Today I am Grateful for ...

_____

_____

_____

_____

_____

_____

_____

_____

_____

Friday 3 June

8 am

_____

_____

10 am

_____

_____

12 pm

_____

_____

2 pm

_____

_____

4 pm

_____

_____

6 pm

_____

_____

_____

July 2011						
M	T	W	T	F	S	S
				1	2	3
4	5	6	7	8	9	10
11	12	13	14	15	16	17
18	19	20	21	22	23	24
25	26	27	28	29	30	31

Today I am Grateful for . . .

Saturday 4 June

Sunday 5 June

Today I am Grateful for . . .

_____

_____

_____

_____

_____

_____

Monday 6 June

8 am

_____

10 am

_____

12 pm

_____

2 pm

_____

4 pm

_____

6 pm

_____

If we make decisions that result in disconnection from God, God does not punish us or become angry. When we come to see that we are the creator of our own life, we will avoid behaviour that hurts us.

AJ Miller

		July 2011				
M	T	W	T	F	S	S
				1	2	3
4	5	6	7	8	9	10
11	12	13	14	15	16	17
18	19	20	21	22	23	24
25	26	27	28	29	30	31

Today I am Grateful for ...

Tuesday 7 June

8 am

10 am

12 pm

2 pm

4 pm

6 pm

Today I am Grateful for . . .

_____

_____

_____

_____

_____

_____

_____

Wednesday 8 June

8 am

10 am

12 pm

2 pm

4 pm

6 pm

		July 2011				
M	T	W	T	F	S	S
				1	2	3
4	5	6	7	8	9	10
11	12	13	14	15	16	17
18	19	20	21	22	23	24
25	26	27	28	29	30	31

Today I am Grateful for . . .

Thursday 9 June

First Quarter Waxing Moon in Virgo
The translation of ideas and concepts to others is all in the details.
Share with others of like mind to clarify your thoughts.

8 am

10 am

12 pm

2 pm

4 pm

6 pm

			May 2011			
M	T	W	T	F	S	S
						1
2	3	4	5	6	7	8
9	10	11	12	13	14	15
16	17	18	19	20	21	22
23	24	25	26	27	28	29
30	31					

Today I am Grateful for . . .

_____
_____
_____
_____
_____
_____
_____
_____

Friday 10 June

8 am
_____
_____

10 am
_____
_____

12 pm
_____
_____

2 pm
_____
_____

4 pm
_____
_____

6 pm
_____
_____

July 2011

M	T	W	T	F	S	S
				1	2	3
4	5	6	7	8	9	10
11	12	13	14	15	16	17
18	19	20	21	22	23	24
25	26	27	28	29	30	31

Today I am Grateful for . . .

Saturday 11 June

Sunday 12 June

Today I am Grateful for . . .

_____
_____
_____
_____
_____
_____
_____
_____

Monday 13 June

8 am
_____
_____

10 am
_____
_____

12 pm
_____
_____

2 pm
_____
_____

4 pm
_____
_____

6 pm
_____
_____

Pain is a great thing because it tells you immediately that something is wrong. Pain tells you when you have broken a law of love.

AJ Miller

		July 2011				
M	T	W	T	F	S	S
				1	2	3
4	5	6	7	8	9	10
11	12	13	14	15	16	17
18	19	20	21	22	23	24
25	26	27	28	29	30	31

Today I am Grateful for . . .

_____

_____

_____

_____

_____

_____

Tuesday 14 June

8 am

_____

10 am

_____

12 pm

_____

2 pm

_____

4 pm

_____

6 pm

_____

			May 2011			
M	T	W	T	F	S	S
						1
2	3	4	5	6	7	8
9	10	11	12	13	14	15
16	17	18	19	20	21	22
23	24	25	26	27	28	29
30	31					

Today I am Grateful for . . .

_____
_____
_____
_____
_____
_____
_____

Wednesday 15 June

8 am
_____
_____

10 am
_____
_____

12 pm
_____
_____

2 pm
_____
_____

4 pm
_____
_____

6 pm
_____
_____

		July 2011				
M	T	W	T	F	S	S
				1	2	3
4	5	6	7	8	9	10
11	12	13	14	15	16	17
18	19	20	21	22	23	24
25	26	27	28	29	30	31

Today I am Grateful for ...

_____

_____

_____

_____

_____

Thursday 16 June

Full Moon in Sagittarius © **Lunar Eclipse** (total) in Sagittarius 24° Sag.
A quiet moment, a thoughtful lull to enjoy some time with friends or family.

8 am

10 am

12 pm

2 pm

4 pm

6 pm

		May 2011				
M	T	W	T	F	S	
						1
2	3	4	5	6	7	8
9	10	11	12	13	14	1
16	17	18	19	20	21	2
23	24	25	26	27	28	2
30	31					

Today I am Grateful for . . .

_____

_____

_____

_____

_____

_____

_____

_____

Friday 17 June

8 am

_____

_____

10 am

_____

_____

12 pm

_____

_____

2 pm

_____

_____

4 pm

_____

_____

6 pm

_____

_____

		July 2011				
M	T	W	T	F	S	S
				1	2	3
4	5	6	7	8	9	10
11	12	13	14	15	16	17
18	19	20	21	22	23	24
25	26	27	28	29	30	31

Today I am Grateful for . . .

_____
_____
_____
_____
_____
_____
_____
_____

Saturday 18 June

_____
_____
_____
_____
_____
_____
_____
_____
_____

Sunday 19 June

_____
_____
_____
_____
_____
_____
_____
_____
_____

Today I am Grateful for . . .

_____

_____

_____

_____

_____

_____

_____

_____

Monday 20 June

8 am

_____

_____

10 am

_____

_____

12 pm

_____

_____

2 pm

_____

_____

4 pm

_____

_____

6 pm

_____

_____

Perhaps all the dragons in our lives are princesses who are only waiting to see us act, just once, with beauty and courage. Perhaps everything that frightens us is, in its deepest essence, something helpless that wants our love.

Rainer Maria Rilke

July 2011

M	T	W	T	F	S	S
				1	2	3
4	5	6	7	8	9	10
11	12	13	14	15	16	17
18	19	20	21	22	23	24
25	26	27	28	29	30	31

Today I am Grateful for . . .

Tuesday 21 June

8 am

10 am

12 pm

2 pm

4 pm

6 pm

		May 2011				
M	T	W	T	F	S	S
						1
2	3	4	5	6	7	8
9	10	11	12	13	14	15
16	17	18	19	20	21	22
23	24	25	26	27	28	29
30	31					

Today I am Grateful for . . .

June Solstice

Attachment versus detachment is a theme that flows through the underlying issues over the next few months. Strive to engage life in a passionate way and find how to balance this with your personal needs and goals. When in doubt remind yourself of the bigger picture and reflect upon what is that endows you with a quality of life.

Wednesday 22 June

8 am

10 am

12 pm

2 pm

4 pm

5 pm

July 2011

M	T	W	T	F	S	S
				1	2	3
4	5	6	7	8	9	10
11	12	13	14	15	16	17
18	19	20	21	22	23	24
25	26	27	28	29	30	31

Today I am Grateful for ...

_____

_____

_____

_____

_____

_____

Thursday 23 June

Third Quarter Waning Moon in Aries
Clarity and inspiration explode into action. This is a high powered time in which to ground your dreams.

8 am

10 am

12 pm

2 pm

4 pm

6 pm

May 2011

M	T	W	T	F	S	S
						1
2	3	4	5	6	7	8
9	10	11	12	13	14	15
16	17	18	19	20	21	22
23	24	25	26	27	28	29
30	31					

Today I am Grateful for . . .

Friday 24 June

8 am

10 am

12 pm

2 pm

4 pm

6 pm

			July 2011			
M	T	W	T	F	S	S
				1	2	3
4	5	6	7	8	9	10
11	12	13	14	15	16	17
18	19	20	21	22	23	24
25	26	27	28	29	30	31

Today I am Grateful for . . .

Saturday 25 June

Sunday 26 June

Today I am Grateful for . . .

_____
_____
_____
_____
_____
_____
_____

Monday 27 June

8 am

_____
_____

10 am

_____
_____

12 pm

_____
_____

2 pm

_____
_____

4 pm

_____
_____

6 pm

_____
_____

All of us will be tempted to deny our own soul condition because we resist that which is painful.

AJ Millar

July 2011

M	T	W	T	F	S	S
				1	2	3
4	5	6	7	8	9	10
11	12	13	14	15	16	17
18	19	20	21	22	23	24
25	26	27	28	29	30	31

Today I am Grateful for ...

_____

_____

_____

_____

_____

Tuesday 28 June

8 am

10 am

12 pm

2 pm

4 pm

6 pm

May 2011

M	T	W	T	F	S	S
						1
2	3	4	5	6	7	8
9	10	11	12	13	14	15
16	17	18	19	20	21	22
23	24	25	26	27	28	29
30	31					

Today I am Grateful for . . .

Wednesday 29 June

8 am

10 am

12 pm

2 pm

4 pm

6 pm

July 2011

M	T	W	T	F	S	S
				1	2	3
4	5	6	7	8	9	10
11	12	13	14	15	16	17
18	19	20	21	22	23	24
25	26	27	28	29	30	31

Today I am Grateful for ...

_____
_____
_____
_____
_____
_____
_____

Thursday 30 June

8 am
_____
_____

10 am
_____
_____

12 pm
_____
_____

2 pm
_____
_____

4 pm
_____
_____

6 pm
_____
_____

May 2011						
M	T	W	T	F	S	S
						1
2	3	4	5	6	7	8
9	10	11	12	13	14	15
16	17	18	19	20	21	22
23	24	25	26	27	28	29
30	31					

Reflections on the Month

Awakening

I knocked on the mountain door
And the mountain let me in.
Only trouble is,
I can't see where it does end
And I begin

I wish I hadn't realised
That what I saw there in its eyes,
Was tenderness
So deep and pure
No other love will I
Ever endure

Renee Searles

July

July 2011

Monday	Tuesday	Wednesday	Thursday	Friday	Saturday	Sunday
				1	2	3
4	5	6	7	8	9	10
11	12	13	14	15	16	17
18	19	20	21	22	23	24
25	26	27	28	29	30	31

Today I am Grateful for ...

◯

_____
_____
_____
_____
_____
_____
_____

New or Dark Moon in Cancer **Solar Eclipse** (partial) in 9° Cancer
_Dynamic and intense energy this month. Resistance helps you to be
cautious as your plans easily fall into place._

Friday 1 July

8 am
_____
_____

10 am
_____
_____

12 pm
_____
_____

2 pm
_____
_____

4 pm
_____
_____

6 pm
_____
_____

August 2011						
M	T	W	T	F	S	S
1	2	3	4	5	6	7
8	9	10	11	12	13	14
15	16	17	18	19	20	21
22	23	24	25	26	27	28
29	30	31				

Today I am Grateful for . . .

_____

_____

_____

_____

_____

_____

_____

Saturday 2 July

_____

_____

_____

_____

_____

_____

_____

_____

_____

Sunday 3 July

_____

_____

_____

_____

_____

_____

_____

_____

_____

_____

Today I am Grateful for . . .

_____
_____
_____
_____
_____
_____
_____

Monday 4 July

8 am
_____

10 am
_____

12 pm
_____

2 pm
_____

4 pm
_____

6 pm
_____

The life that is unexamined is not worth living.

Plato

August 2011

M	T	W	T	F	S	S
1	2	3	4	5	6	7
8	9	10	11	12	13	14
15	16	17	18	19	20	21
22	23	24	25	26	27	28
29	30	31				

Today I am Grateful for . . .

_____

_____

_____

_____

_____

Tuesday 5 July

8 am
_____

10 am
_____

12 pm
_____

2 pm
_____

4 pm
_____

6 pm
_____

		June 2011				
M	T	W	T	F	S	S
		1	2	3	4	5
6	7	8	9	10	11	12
13	14	15	16	17	18	19
20	21	22	23	24	25	26
27	28	29	30			

Today I am Grateful for ...

_____
_____
_____
_____
_____
_____
_____
_____

Wednesday 6 July

8 am
_____
_____

10 am
_____
_____

12 pm
_____
_____

2 pm
_____
_____

4 pm
_____
_____

6 pm
_____
_____

August 2011						
M	T	W	T	F	S	S
1	2	3	4	5	6	7
8	9	10	11	12	13	14
15	16	17	18	19	20	21
22	23	24	25	26	27	28
29	30	31				

Today I am Grateful for . . .

_____

_____

_____

_____

_____

_____

Thursday 7 July

8 am

_____

10 am

_____

12 pm

_____

2 pm

_____

4 pm

_____

6 pm

_____

			June 2011			
M	T	W	T	F	S	
		1	2	3	4	5
6	7	8	9	10	11	12
13	14	15	16	17	18	19
20	21	22	23	24	25	26
27	28	29	30			

Today I am Grateful for . . .

_____
_____
_____
_____
_____
_____
_____
_____

First Quarter Waxing Moon in Libra
Brilliant time to strategise and resolve issues into win/win solutions for all.

Friday 8 July

8 am

10 am

12 pm

2 pm

4 pm

6 pm

August 2011

M	T	W	T	F	S	S
1	2	3	4	5	6	7
8	9	10	11	12	13	14
15	16	17	18	19	20	21
22	23	24	25	26	27	28
29	30	31				

Today I am Grateful for . . .

Saturday 9 July

Sunday 10 July

Today I am Grateful for . . .

_____
_____
_____
_____
_____
_____
_____

Monday 11 July

8 am
_____
_____

10 am
_____
_____

12 pm
_____
_____

2 pm
_____
_____

4 pm
_____
_____

6 pm
_____
_____

Abundance can be had by simply consciously receiving what has already been given.

Sufi proverb

August 2011

M	T	W	T	F	S	S
1	2	3	4	5	6	7
8	9	10	11	12	13	14
15	16	17	18	19	20	21
22	23	24	25	26	27	28
29	30	31				

Today I am Grateful for . . .

_____

_____

_____

_____

_____

_____

Tuesday 12 July

8 am

_____

10 am

_____

12 pm

_____

2 pm

_____

4 pm

_____

6 pm

_____

			June 2011			
M	T	W	T	F	S	
		1	2	3	4	5
6	7	8	9	10	11	12
13	14	15	16	17	18	19
20	21	22	23	24	25	26
27	28	29	30			

Today I am Grateful for . . .

_____

_____

_____

_____

_____

_____

_____

_____

Wednesday 13 July

8 am

10 am

12 pm

2 pm

4 pm

6 pm

August 2011

M	T	W	T	F	S	S
1	2	3	4	5	6	7
8	9	10	11	12	13	14
15	16	17	18	19	20	21
22	23	24	25	26	27	28
29	30	31				

Today I am Grateful for ...

_____
_____
_____
_____
_____
_____

Thursday 14 July

8 am
_____

10 am
_____

12 pm
_____

2 pm
_____

4 pm
_____

6 pm
_____

June 2011

M	T	W	T	F	S
		1	2	3	4
6	7	8	9	10	11
13	14	15	16	17	18
20	21	22	23	24	25
27	28	29	30		

Today I am Grateful for ...

Friday 15 July

3 am

10 am

12 pm

2 pm

4 pm

5 pm

Full Moon in Capricorn
After an intense week a little time to recoup one's energy is necessary. Deep sharing with those closest to you will also bring its rewards

August 2011

M	T	W	T	F	S	S
1	2	3	4	5	6	7
8	9	10	11	12	13	14
15	16	17	18	19	20	21
22	23	24	25	26	27	28
29	30	31				

Today I am Grateful for . . .

Saturday 16 July

Sunday 17 July

Today I am Grateful for . . .

_____

_____

_____

_____

_____

_____

Monday 18 July

am

_____

0 am

_____

2 pm

_____

pm

_____

pm

_____

pm

_____

People are like stained glass windows. They sparkle
and shine when the sun is out, but when the darkness
sets in, their true beauty is revealed only if there is
a light from within.

Elisabeth Kübler-Ross

August 2011

M	T	W	T	F	S	S
1	2	3	4	5	6	7
8	9	10	11	12	13	14
15	16	17	18	19	20	21
22	23	24	25	26	27	28
29	30	31				

Today I am Grateful for ...

_____

_____

_____

_____

_____

_____

Tuesday 19 July

8 am

_____

10 am

_____

12 pm

_____

2 pm

_____

4 pm

_____

6 pm

_____

		June 2011			
M	T	W	T	F	S
		1	2	3	4
6	7	8	9	10	11
13	14	15	16	17	18
20	21	22	23	24	25
27	28	29	30		

Today I am Grateful for . . .

_____

_____

_____

_____

_____

_____

Wednesday 20 July

8 am

_____

_____

10 am

_____

_____

12 pm

_____

_____

2 pm

_____

_____

4 pm

_____

_____

6 pm

_____

_____

_____

| August 2011 | | | | | | |
M	T	W	T	F	S	S
1	2	3	4	5	6	7
8	9	10	11	12	13	14
15	16	17	18	19	20	21
22	23	24	25	26	27	28
29	30	31				

Today I am Grateful for . . .

_____

_____

_____

_____

_____

_____

Thursday 21 July

8 am

_____

10 am

_____

12 pm

_____

2 pm

_____

4 pm

_____

6 pm

_____

June 2011

M	T	W	T	F	S	
		1	2	3	4	5
6	7	8	9	10	11	12
13	14	15	16	17	18	19
20	21	22	23	24	25	26
27	28	29	30			

Today I am Grateful for . . .

_____

_____

_____

_____

_____

_____

_____

_____

Friday 22 July

8 am
_____

_____

10 am
_____

_____

12 pm
_____

_____

2 pm
_____

_____

4 pm
_____

_____

6 pm
_____

_____

		August 2011				
M	T	W	T	F	S	S
1	2	3	4	5	6	7
8	9	10	11	12	13	14
15	16	17	18	19	20	21
22	23	24	25	26	27	28
29	30	31				

Today I am Grateful for . . .

Saturday 23 July

Third Quarter Waning Moon in Taurus
A feeling of confidence revitalises the soul as you review and take stock of your achievements or journey this past year. A good week for entertainment.

Sunday 24 July

Today I am Grateful for . . .

_____
_____
_____
_____
_____
_____
_____
_____

Monday 25 July

8 am
_____
_____
_____

10 am
_____
_____
_____

12 pm
_____
_____
_____

2 pm
_____
_____
_____

4 pm
_____
_____
_____

6 pm
_____
_____
_____

To everyone who has, more shall be given
And he shall have an abundance;
But from the one that does not have,
Even that which he has shall be taken from him.

Matthew 25:29

August 2011

M	T	W	T	F	S	S
1	2	3	4	5	6	7
8	9	10	11	12	13	14
15	16	17	18	19	20	21
22	23	24	25	26	27	28
29	30	31				

Today I am Grateful for . . .

_____

_____

_____

_____

_____

_____

Tuesday 26 July

8 am

10 am

12 pm

2 pm

4 pm

6 pm

June 2011

M	T	W	T	F	S	S
		1	2	3	4	5
6	7	8	9	10	11	12
13	14	15	16	17	18	19
20	21	22	23	24	25	26
27	28	29	30			

Today I am Grateful for . . .

_____

_____

_____

_____

_____

_____

_____

Wednesday 27 July

8 am

_____

_____

10 am

_____

_____

12 pm

_____

_____

2 pm

_____

_____

4 pm

_____

_____

6 pm

_____

_____

August 2011						
M	T	W	T	F	S	S
1	2	3	4	5	6	7
8	9	10	11	12	13	14
15	16	17	18	19	20	21
22	23	24	25	26	27	28
29	30	31				

Today I am Grateful for ...

Thursday 28 July

8 am

10 am

12 pm

2 pm

4 pm

6 pm

June 2011

M	T	W	T	F	S	S
		1	2	3	4	5
6	7	8	9	10	11	1
13	14	15	16	17	18	1
20	21	22	23	24	25	2
27	28	29	30			

Today I am Grateful for . . .

_____
_____
_____
_____
_____
_____
_____
_____

Friday 29 July

8 am
_____
_____

10 am
_____
_____

12 pm
_____
_____

2 pm
_____
_____

4 pm
_____
_____

6 pm
_____
_____

August 2011						
M	T	W	T	F	S	S
1	2	3	4	5	6	7
8	9	10	11	12	13	14
15	16	17	18	19	20	21
22	23	24	25	26	27	28
29	30	31				

Today I am Grateful for . . .

Saturday 30 July

New or Dark Moon in Leo
A new revitalised self with the ability to be present and shine from the heart emerges as changes continue to affect many areas of your life.

Sunday 31 July

Reflections on the Month

Soulmates

Because the one I love lives inside of you,
I will always lean as close to your body
as I can
And I think of you all the time, dear
pilgrim,
Because the one I love goes with you.

August

Photo by Mario Mat

August 2011

Monday	Tuesday	Wednesday	Thursday	Friday	Saturday	Sunday
1	2	3	4	5	6	7
8	9	10	11	12	13	14
15	16	17	18	19	20	21
22	23	24	25	26	27	28
29	30	31				

Today I am Grateful for . . .

_____
_____
_____
_____
_____
_____
_____

Monday 1 August

am
_____

_____

0 am
_____

_____

2 pm
_____

_____

pm
_____

_____

pm
_____

_____

pm
_____

_____

**have fallen in love many times …
always with you.**

Anon

		September 2011				
M	T	W	T	F	S	S
			1	2	3	4
5	6	7	8	9	10	11
12	13	14	15	16	17	18
19	20	21	22	23	24	25
26	27	28	29	30		

Today I am Grateful for ...

Tuesday 2 August

8 am

10 am

12 pm

2 pm

4 pm

6 pm

		July 2011			
M	T	W	T	F	S
				1	2
4	5	6	7	8	9
11	12	13	14	15	16
18	19	20	21	22	23
25	26	27	28	29	30

Today I am Grateful for . . .

_____

_____

_____

_____

_____

_____

_____

Wednesday 3 August

8 am

_____

_____

10 am

_____

_____

12 pm

_____

_____

2 pm

_____

_____

4 pm

_____

_____

5 pm

_____

_____

_____

		September 2011				
M	T	W	T	F	S	S
			1	2	3	4
5	6	7	8	9	10	11
12	13	14	15	16	17	18
19	20	21	22	23	24	25
26	27	28	29	30		

Today I am Grateful for . . .

_____

_____

_____

_____

_____

_____

Thursday 4 August

8 am

_____

10 am

_____

12 pm

_____

2 pm

_____

4 pm

_____

6 pm

_____

**I feel you coming
like a planet slowly turning
like a dervish softly whirling
like a new born fern unfurling.**
Renee Searles

July 2011

M	T	W	T	F	S	S
				1	2	3
4	5	6	7	8	9	10
11	12	13	14	15	16	17
18	19	20	21	22	23	24
25	26	27	28	29	30	31

Today I am Grateful for . . .

_____
_____
_____
_____
_____
_____

Friday 5 August

8 am
_____

_____

10 am
_____

_____

12 pm
_____

_____

2 pm
_____

_____

4 pm
_____

_____

6 pm
_____

_____

| | September 2011 | | | | | |
M	T	W	T	F	S	S
			1	2	3	4
5	6	7	8	9	10	11
12	13	14	15	16	17	18
19	20	21	22	23	24	25
26	27	28	29	30		

Today I am Grateful for . . .

Saturday 6 August

First Quarter Waxing Moon in Scorpio
Focus on your goals as anything is possible. Even as the groundwork is being laid there is still time for review. Be generous in your attitude and helpful to others. People and relationships are important.

Sunday 7 August

Today I am Grateful for . . .

_____
_____
_____
_____
_____
_____
_____

Monday 8 August

8 am
_____
_____

10 am
_____
_____

12 pm
_____
_____

2 pm
_____
_____

4 pm
_____
_____

6 pm
_____
_____

You will not find a soulmate in the quiet of your room; you must go to a noisy place and look in the quiet corners.

Robert Brault

September 2011

M	T	W	T	F	S	S
			1	2	3	4
5	6	7	8	9	10	11
12	13	14	15	16	17	18
19	20	21	22	23	24	25
26	27	28	29	30		

Today I am Grateful for . . .

_____

Tuesday 9 August

8 am

10 am

12 pm

2 pm

4 pm

6 pm

July 2011

M	T	W	T	F	S	S
				1	2	3
4	5	6	7	8	9	10
11	12	13	14	15	16	17
18	19	20	21	22	23	24
25	26	27	28	29	30	31

Today I am Grateful for . . .

_____
_____
_____
_____
_____
_____
_____

Wednesday 10 August

8 am
_____
_____

10 am
_____
_____

12 pm
_____
_____

2 pm
_____
_____

4 pm
_____
_____

6 pm
_____
_____

September 2011						
M	T	W	T	F	S	S
			1	2	3	4
5	6	7	8	9	10	11
12	13	14	15	16	17	18
19	20	21	22	23	24	25
26	27	28	29	30		

Today I am Grateful for . . .

_____

_____

_____

_____

_____

_____

Thursday 11 August

8 am

10 am

12 pm

2 pm

4 pm

6 pm

	July 2011					
M	T	W	T	F	S	S
				1	2	3
4	5	6	7	8	9	10
11	12	13	14	15	16	17
18	19	20	21	22	23	24
25	26	27	28	29	30	31

Today I am Grateful for . . .

_____

_____

_____

_____

_____

_____

Friday 12 August

8 am
_____

_____

10 am
_____

_____

12 pm
_____

_____

2 pm
_____

_____

4 pm
_____

_____

6 pm
_____

_____

September 2011						
M	T	W	T	F	S	S
			1	2	3	4
5	6	7	8	9	10	11
12	13	14	15	16	17	18
19	20	21	22	23	24	25
26	27	28	29	30		

Today I am Grateful for . . .

Saturday 13 August

Full Moon in Aquarius
A selfless time that is much more about giving than it is about receiving. Let go of control and allow time to sit in the compassionate self.

Sunday 14 August

Today I am Grateful for . . .

_____

_____

_____

_____

_____

_____

_____

Monday 15 August

8 am
_____

_____

10 am
_____

_____

12 pm
_____

_____

2 pm
_____

_____

4 pm
_____

_____

5 pm
_____

_____

I shall wait patiently
Like a monolithic tomb
Like a song without its tune
Like a baby
In her womb.

Renee Searles, 'To Me'

September 2011

M	T	W	T	F	S	S
			1	2	3	4
5	6	7	8	9	10	11
12	13	14	15	16	17	18
19	20	21	22	23	24	25
26	27	28	29	30		

Today I am Grateful for . . .

_____

_____

_____

_____

_____

_____

Tuesday 16 August

8 am

_____

10 am

_____

12 pm

_____

2 pm

_____

4 pm

_____

6 pm

_____

		July 2011				
M	T	W	T	F	S	
				1	2	3
4	5	6	7	8	9	10
11	12	13	14	15	16	17
18	19	20	21	22	23	24
25	26	27	28	29	30	31

Today I am Grateful for . . .

_____

_____

_____

_____

_____

_____

_____

_____

Wednesday 17 August

8 am

_____

10 am

_____

12 pm

_____

2 pm

_____

4 pm

_____

6 pm

_____

		September 2011				
M	T	W	T	F	S	S
			1	2	3	4
5	6	7	8	9	10	11
12	13	14	15	16	17	18
19	20	21	22	23	24	25
26	27	28	29	30		

Today I am Grateful for . . .

_____
_____
_____
_____
_____
_____

Thursday 18 August

8 am
_____

10 am
_____

12 pm
_____

2 pm
_____

4 pm
_____

6 pm
_____

Oh come my love
Don't you fear,
Eons of heartbeats
Have brought you here.
Renee Searles 'To Me'

			July 2011			
M	T	W	T	F	S	S
				1	2	3
4	5	6	7	8	9	10
11	12	13	14	15	16	17
18	19	20	21	22	23	24
25	26	27	28	29	30	31

Today I am Grateful for ...

_____
_____
_____
_____
_____
_____
_____

Friday 19 August

8 am
_____
_____

10 am
_____
_____

12 pm
_____
_____

pm
_____
_____

pm
_____
_____

pm
_____

September 2011

M	T	W	T	F	S	S
			1	2	3	4
5	6	7	8	9	10	11
12	13	14	15	16	17	18
19	20	21	22	23	24	25
26	27	28	29	30		

Today I am Grateful for . . .

Saturday 20 August

Sunday 21 August

Today I am Grateful for . . .

Third Quarter Waning Moon in Taurus
Working with others towards a shared task brings peace into your heart. Be clear with your communications.

Monday 22 August

8 am

10 am

12 pm

2 pm

4 pm

6 pm

September 2011

M	T	W	T	F	S	S
			1	2	3	4
5	6	7	8	9	10	11
12	13	14	15	16	17	18
19	20	21	22	23	24	25
26	27	28	29	30		

How does one recognise a soulmate?
Well, how do you know yourself?
Would you recognise yourself if you met yourself
in the hallway?

Saint Germain

Today I am Grateful for . . .

Tuesday 23 August

8 am

10 am

12 pm

2 pm

4 pm

6 pm

July 2011

M	T	W	T	F	S	S
				1	2	3
4	5	6	7	8	9	10
11	12	13	14	15	16	17
18	19	20	21	22	23	24
25	26	27	28	29	30	31

Today I am Grateful for . . .

_____
_____
_____
_____
_____
_____

Wednesday 24 August

8 am
_____
_____

10 am
_____
_____

12 pm
_____
_____

2 pm
_____
_____

4 pm
_____
_____

6 pm
_____
_____

September 2011

M	T	W	T	F	S	S
			1	2	3	4
5	6	7	8	9	10	11
12	13	14	15	16	17	18
19	20	21	22	23	24	25
26	27	28	29	30		

Today I am Grateful for . . .

_____
_____
_____
_____
_____
_____

Thursday 25 August

8 am
_____
_____

10 am
_____
_____

12 pm
_____
_____

2 pm
_____
_____

4 pm
_____
_____

6 pm
_____
_____

July 2011

M	T	W	T	F	S	S
				1	2	3
4	5	6	7	8	9	10
11	12	13	14	15	16	17
18	19	20	21	22	23	24
25	26	27	28	29	30	31

Today I am Grateful for . . .

_____

_____

_____

_____

_____

_____

_____

_____

Friday 26 August

8 am

10 am

12 pm

2 pm

4 pm

6 pm

September 2011

M	T	W	T	F	S	S
			1	2	3	4
5	6	7	8	9	10	11
12	13	14	15	16	17	18
19	20	21	22	23	24	25
26	27	28	29	30		

Today I am Grateful for . . .

Saturday 27 August

Sunday 28 August

Today I am Grateful for . . .

○

_____

_____

_____

_____

_____

_____

New or Dark Moon in Virgo
Life is good. Make a list of everything that you have achieved and manifested in your life and give thanks.

Monday 29 August

8 am

_____

10 am

_____

12 pm

_____

2 pm

_____

4 pm

_____

6 pm

_____

In a soulmate we find not company but a completed solitude.

Robert Brault

September 2011

M	T	W	T	F	S	S
			1	2	3	4
5	6	7	8	9	10	11
12	13	14	15	16	17	18
19	20	21	22	23	24	25
26	27	28	29	30		

Today I am Grateful for . . .

_____

_____

_____

_____

_____

_____

Tuesday 30 August

8 am

10 am

12 pm

2 pm

4 pm

6 pm

		July 2011				
M	T	W	T	F	S	
				1	2	3
4	5	6	7	8	9	10
11	12	13	14	15	16	17
18	19	20	21	22	23	24
25	26	27	28	29	30	31

Today I am Grateful for . . .

_____
_____
_____
_____
_____
_____
_____

Wednesday 31 August

8 am
_____
_____

10 am
_____
_____

12 pm
_____
_____

2 pm
_____
_____

4 pm
_____
_____

6 pm
_____
_____

		September 2011				
M	T	W	T	F	S	S
			1	2	3	4
5	6	7	8	9	10	11
12	13	14	15	16	17	18
19	20	21	22	23	24	25
26	27	28	29	30		

Reflections on the Month

Reflections on the Month

Trust

September

The best way to find out if you can trust somebody is to trust them.

Ernest Hemingway

September 2011

Monday	Tuesday	Wednesday	Thursday	Friday	Saturday	Sunday
			1	2	3	4
5	6	7	8	9	10	11
12	13	14	15	16	17	18
19	20	21	22	23	24	25
26	27	28	29	30		

Today I am Grateful for ...

_____

_____

_____

_____

_____

_____

_____

Thursday 1 September

8 am

_____

_____

10 am

_____

_____

12 pm

_____

_____

2 pm

_____

_____

4 pm

_____

_____

6 pm

_____

_____

| October 2011 | | | | | | |
M	T	W	T	F	S	S
					1	2
3	4	5	6	7	8	9
10	11	12	13	14	15	16
17	18	19	20	21	22	23
24	25	26	27	28	29	30
31						

Today I am Grateful for ...

_____
_____
_____
_____
_____
_____

Friday 2 September

8 am
_____
_____

10 am
_____
_____

12 pm
_____
_____

2 pm
_____
_____

4 pm
_____
_____

6 pm
_____
_____

August 2011						
M	T	W	T	F	S	S
1	2	3	4	5	6	7
8	9	10	11	12	13	14
15	16	17	18	19	20	21
22	23	24	25	26	27	28
29	30	31				

Today I am Grateful for . . .

Saturday 3 September

Sunday 4 September

Today I am Grateful for ...

_____
_____
_____
_____
_____
_____

Monday 5 September

First Quarter Waxing Moon in Sagittarius
A restless week waiting for clarity. Be patient and wait for irrefutable signs regarding which way to move forward.

8 am

10 am

12 pm

2 pm

4 pm

6 pm

By letting go it all gets done
The world is won by those who let it go,
But when you try and try,
The world is beyond the winning.
Lao Tzu

August 2011						
M	T	W	T	F	S	S
1	2	3	4	5	6	7
8	9	10	11	12	13	14
15	16	17	18	19	20	21
22	23	24	25	26	27	28
29	30	31				

Today I am Grateful for . . .

_____
_____
_____
_____
_____
_____
_____

Tuesday 6 September

8 am
_____
_____

10 am
_____
_____

12 pm
_____
_____

2 pm
_____
_____

4 pm
_____
_____

6 pm
_____
_____

October 2011

M	T	W	T	F	S	S
					1	2
3	4	5	6	7	8	9
10	11	12	13	14	15	16
17	18	19	20	21	22	23
24	25	26	27	28	29	30
31						

Today I am Grateful for . . .

_____

_____

_____

_____

_____

Wednesday 7 September

8 am

_____

10 am

_____

12 pm

_____

2 pm

_____

4 pm

_____

6 pm

_____

August 2011						
M	T	W	T	F	S	S
1	2	3	4	5	6	7
8	9	10	11	12	13	14
15	16	17	18	19	20	21
22	23	24	25	26	27	28
29	,30	31				

Today I am Grateful for . . .

_____
_____
_____
_____
_____
_____
_____

Thursday 8 September

8 am
_____
_____

10 am
_____
_____

12 pm
_____
_____

2 pm
_____
_____

4 pm
_____
_____

6 pm
_____
_____

October 2011

M	T	W	T	F	S	S
					1	2
3	4	5	6	7	8	9
10	11	12	13	14	15	16
17	18	19	20	21	22	23
24	25	26	27	28	29	30
31						

Today I am Grateful for . . .

_____

_____

_____

_____

_____

_____

Friday 9 September

8 am

_____

10 am

_____

12 pm

_____

2 pm

_____

4 pm

_____

6 pm

_____

		August 2011				
M	T	W	T	F	S	S
1	2	3	4	5	6	7
8	9	10	11	12	13	14
15	16	17	18	19	20	21
22	23	24	25	26	27	28
29	30	31				

Today I am Grateful for . . .

Saturday 10 September

Sunday 11 September

Today I am Grateful for . . .

_____

_____

_____

_____

_____

_____

Full Moon in Pisces
Continue to surrender and trust and take each step as it appears.
There are large shifts in consciousness seeding so the best you can do
is to remain present with your everyday activities. Dinner with friends
and sharing a few stories will be rewarding.

Monday 12 September

8 am

10 am

12 pm

2 pm

4 pm

6 pm

We try to love where trust has been broken,
but we can easily love without trusting as we
can hug without embracing.

Robert Brault

August 2011

M	T	W	T	F	S	S
1	2	3	4	5	6	7
8	9	10	11	12	13	14
15	16	17	18	19	20	21
22	23	24	25	26	27	28
29	30	31				

Today I am Grateful for ...

Tuesday 13 September

8 am

10 am

12 pm

2 pm

4 pm

6 pm

October 2011

M	T	W	T	F	S	S
					1	2
3	4	5	6	7	8	9
10	11	12	13	14	15	16
17	18	19	20	21	22	23
24	25	26	27	28	29	30
31						

Today I am Grateful for ...

_____

_____

_____

_____

_____

_____

Wednesday 14 September

8 am
_____

_____

10 am
_____

_____

12 pm
_____

_____

2 pm
_____

_____

4 pm
_____

_____

6 pm
_____

_____

		August 2011				
M	T	W	T	F	S	S
1	2	3	4	5	6	7
8	9	10	11	12	13	14
15	16	17	18	19	20	21
22	23	24	25	26	27	28
29	30	31				

Today I am Grateful for . . .

_____
_____
_____
_____
_____
_____
_____
_____

Thursday 15 September

am
_____
_____

0 am
_____
_____

2 pm
_____
_____

pm
_____
_____

pm
_____
_____

pm
_____
_____

October 2011

M	T	W	T	F	S	S
					1	2
3	4	5	6	7	8	9
10	11	12	13	14	15	16
17	18	19	20	21	22	23
24	25	26	27	28	29	30
31						

Today I am Grateful for . . .

Friday 16 September

8 am

10 am

12 pm

2 pm

4 pm

6 pm

August 2011						
M	T	W	T	F	S	S
1	2	3	4	5	6	7
8	9	10	11	12	13	14
15	16	17	18	19	20	21
22	23	24	25	26	27	28
29	30	31				

Today I am Grateful for ...

Saturday 17 September

Sunday 18 September

Today I am Grateful for . . .

_____

_____

_____

_____

_____

_____

Monday 19 September

8 am

_____

10 am

_____

12 pm

_____

2 pm

_____

4 pm

_____

6 pm

_____

Remember, truth is an emotional process.
It is not an intellectual one.
The more strongly you desire truth,
The more it will come into your life.

AJ Miller

August 2011

M	T	W	T	F	S	S
1	2	3	4	5	6	7
8	9	10	11	12	13	14
15	16	17	18	19	20	21
22	23	24	25	26	27	28
29	30	31				

Today I am Grateful for ...

_____
_____
_____
_____
_____
_____
_____
_____

Tuesday 20 September

Third Quarter Waning Moon in Gemini
Busy, busy, busy at work, at home, with friends and family. Life is meant to be enjoyed so laugh a little when it's not perfect.

8 am
_____
_____

10 am
_____
_____

12 pm
_____
_____

2 pm
_____
_____

4 pm
_____
_____

6 pm
_____
_____

	October 2011					
M	T	W	T	F	S	S
					1	2
3	4	5	6	7	8	9
10	11	12	13	14	15	16
17	18	19	20	21	22	23
24	25	26	27	28	29	30
31						

Today I am Grateful for . . .

_____

_____

_____

_____

_____

Wednesday 21 September

8 am
_____

_____

10 am
_____

_____

12 pm
_____

_____

2 pm
_____

_____

4 pm
_____

_____

6 pm
_____

_____

		August 2011				
M	T	W	T	F	S	S
1	2	3	4	5	6	7
8	9	10	11	12	13	14
15	16	17	18	19	20	21
22	23	24	25	26	27	28
29	30	31				

Today I am Grateful for . . .

_____
_____
_____
_____
_____
_____
_____
_____

September Equinox
The preservation of our world must take us beyond thoughts limited by our individual desires. Joining forces with others of like-minded views and passions helps to anchor the collective desire to keep the beauty of our planet and the best of the many cultures inhabiting our world intact.

Thursday 22 September

8 am
_____

10 am
_____

12 pm
_____

2 pm
_____

4 pm
_____

6 pm
_____

October 2011

M	T	W	T	F	S	S
					1	2
3	4	5	6	7	8	9
10	11	12	13	14	15	16
17	18	19	20	21	22	23
24	25	26	27	28	29	30
31						

Today I am Grateful for . . .

_____

_____

_____

_____

_____

_____

Friday 23 September

8 am

_____

10 am

_____

12 pm

_____

2 pm

_____

4 pm

_____

6 pm

_____

		August 2011				
M	T	W	T	F	S	S
1	2	3	4	5	6	7
8	9	10	11	12	13	14
15	16	17	18	19	20	21
22	23	24	25	26	27	28
29	30	31				

Today I am Grateful for . . .

Saturday 24 September

Sunday 25 September

Today I am Grateful for . . .

_____

_____

_____

_____

_____

_____

Monday 26 September

8 am

_____

10 am

_____

12 pm

_____

2 pm

_____

4 pm

_____

6 pm

_____

**Sometimes regretted more than any words spoken
is a silence not broken.**

Robert Brault

August 2011

M	T	W	T	F	S	S
1	2	3	4	5	6	7
8	9	10	11	12	13	14
15	16	17	18	19	20	21
22	23	24	25	26	27	28
29	30	31				

Today I am Grateful for ...

◯

Tuesday 27 September

3 am

10 am

12 pm

2 pm

4 pm

6 pm

New or Dark Moon in Libra
This moon cycle brings wisdom and clarity as well as the ability to choose well. Thoughtful decisions that incorporate the new without destroying the old are supported. Strive to keep a balance between feminine wisdom and masculine discipline.

October 2011

M	T	W	T	F	S	S
					1	2
3	4	5	6	7	8	9
10	11	12	13	14	15	16
17	18	19	20	21	22	23
24	25	26	27	28	29	30
31						

Today I am Grateful for ...

_____

_____

_____

_____

_____

Wednesday 28 September

8 am

10 am

12 pm

2 pm

4 pm

6 pm

August 2011

M	T	W	T	F	S	S
1	2	3	4	5	6	7
8	9	10	11	12	13	14
15	16	17	18	19	20	21
22	23	24	25	26	27	28
29	30	31				

Today I am Grateful for . . .

_____
_____
_____
_____
_____
_____
_____

Thursday 29 September

8 am
_____
_____

10 am
_____
_____

12 pm
_____
_____

2 pm
_____
_____

4 pm
_____
_____

6 pm
_____
_____

| October 2011 | | | | | | |
M	T	W	T	F	S	S
					1	2
3	4	5	6	7	8	9
10	11	12	13	14	15	16
17	18	19	20	21	22	23
24	25	26	27	28	29	30
31						

Today I am Grateful for . . .

_____

_____

_____

_____

_____

_____

Friday 30 September

8 am
_____

_____

10 am
_____

_____

12 pm
_____

_____

2 pm
_____

_____

4 pm
_____

_____

6 pm
_____

_____

| August 2011 | | | | | | |
M	T	W	T	F	S	S
1	2	3	4	5	6	7
8	9	10	11	12	13	14
15	16	17	18	19	20	21
22	23	24	25	26	27	28
29	30	31				

Reflections on the Month

Love

We are worthy of love

Any feeling that we are not good enough, unworthy, unloved by God, alone in this world, unable to be forgiven ... are emotions of error which will prevent Her love from flowing to us. We need to understand that a part of worthiness is to validate and experience our own emotions. Each time we release. If we pray to God for Love, these dormant feelings no longer block God's love.

AJ Miller

October

October 2011

Monday	Tuesday	Wednesday	Thursday	Friday	Saturday	Sunday
					1	2
3	4	5	6	7	8	9
10	11	12	13	14	15	16
17	18	19	20	21	22	23
24	25	26	27	28	29	30
31						

Today I am Grateful for . . .

Saturday 1 October

Sunday 2 October

Today I am Grateful for . . .

_____
_____
_____
_____
_____
_____

Monday 3 October

8 am
_____
_____
_____

10 am
_____
_____
_____

12 pm
_____
_____
_____

2 pm
_____
_____
_____

4 pm
_____
_____
_____

6 pm
_____
_____
_____

**Love and kindness are never wasted. They always
make a difference. They bless the one who receives
them, and they bless you, the giver.**

Barbara De Angelis

September 2011

M	T	W	T	F	S	S
			1	2	3	4
5	6	7	8	9	10	11
12	13	14	15	16	17	18
19	20	21	22	23	24	25
26	27	28	29	30		

Today I am Grateful for . . .

_____

_____

_____

_____

_____

_____

_____

First Quarter Waxing Moon in *Capricorn*
Moving through a little resistance is good for the soul. Trust your instincts as your path continues to open up before you.

Tuesday 4 October

8 am

10 am

12 pm

2 pm

4 pm

6 pm

November 2011

M	T	W	T	F	S	S
	1	2	3	4	5	6
7	8	9	10	11	12	13
14	15	16	17	18	19	20
21	22	23	24	25	26	27
28	29	30				

Today I am Grateful for . . .

_____

_____

_____

_____

_____

Wednesday 5 October

8 am

_____

10 am

_____

12 pm

_____

2 pm

_____

4 pm

_____

6 pm

_____

September 2011

M	T	W	T	F	S	S
			1	2	3	4
5	6	7	8	9	10	11
12	13	14	15	16	17	18
19	20	21	22	23	24	25
26	27	28	29	30		

God desires our Love . . .

_____
_____
_____
_____
_____
_____

Thursday 6 October

8 am
_____
_____

10 am
_____
_____

12 pm
_____
_____

2 pm
_____
_____

4 pm
_____
_____

6 pm
_____
_____

November 2011						
M	T	W	T	F	S	S
	1	2	3	4	5	6
7	8	9	10	11	12	13
14	15	16	17	18	19	20
21	22	23	24	25	26	27
28	29	30				

Today I am Grateful for . . .

Friday 7 October

8 am

10 am

12 pm

2 pm

4 pm

6 pm

September 2011

M	T	W	T	F	S	S
			1	2	3	4
5	6	7	8	9	10	11
12	13	14	15	16	17	18
19	20	21	22	23	24	25
26	27	28	29	30		

Today I am Grateful for . . .

Saturday 8 October

Sunday 9 October

Today I am Grateful for . . .

Monday 10 October

8 am

10 am

12 pm

2 pm

4 pm

6 pm

Love is patient, love is kind.
It does not envy, it does not boast, it is not proud.
It is not rude, it is not self-seeking.
It is not easily angered, it keeps no record of wrongs.
Love does not delight in evil, but rejoices with the truth.
It always protects, always trusts, always hopes, always perseveres.
Love never fails.

1 Corinthians 13:4-8

September 2011

M	T	W	T	F	S	S
			1	2	3	4
5	6	7	8	9	10	11
12	13	14	15	16	17	18
19	20	21	22	23	24	25
26	27	28	29	30		

Today I am Grateful for . . .

Tuesday 11 October

8 am

10 am

12 pm

2 pm

4 pm

6 pm

November 2011						
M	T	W	T	F	S	S
	1	2	3	4	5	6
7	8	9	10	11	12	13
14	15	16	17	18	19	20
21	22	23	24	25	26	27
28	29	30				

Today I am Grateful for ...

_____

_____

_____

_____

_____

_____

Wednesday 12 October

Full Moon in Aries
Being true to your self is not always easy but it can give a unique experience of profound freedom. Be careful not to let the needs of others disempower your choices.

8 am

10 am

12 pm

2 pm

4 pm

6 pm

September 2011

M	T	W	T	F	S	S
			1	2	3	4
5	6	7	8	9	10	11
12	13	14	15	16	17	18
19	20	21	22	23	24	25
26	27	28	29	30		

Do I Feel Worthy of God's Love?

_____

_____

_____

_____

_____

_____

Thursday 13 October

8 am
_____

_____

10 am
_____

_____

12 pm
_____

_____

2 pm
_____

_____

4 pm
_____

_____

6 pm
_____

_____

_____

November 2011						
M	T	W	T	F	S	S
	1	2	3	4	5	6
7	8	9	10	11	12	13
14	15	16	17	18	19	20
21	22	23	24	25	26	27
28	29	30				

Today I am Grateful for . . .

_____

_____

_____

_____

_____

_____

Friday 14 October

8 am
_____

_____

10 am
_____

_____

12 pm
_____

_____

2 pm
_____

_____

4 pm
_____

_____

6 pm
_____

_____

September 2011

M	T	W	T	F	S	S
			1	2	3	4
5	6	7	8	9	10	11
12	13	14	15	16	17	18
19	20	21	22	23	24	25
26	27	28	29	30		

Today I am Grateful for . . .

Saturday 15 October

Sunday 16 October

Today I am Grateful for . . .

_____
_____
_____
_____
_____

Monday 17 October

8 am
_____

_____

10 am
_____

_____

12 pm
_____

_____

2 pm
_____

_____

4 pm
_____

_____

6 pm
_____

_____

God's love and God called love is defined that God brought forth you into life. It has given you life and has never taken it away from you, so if God is love then the secret is the act of giving without conditions. Taking doesn't mean love; it's giving that means it.

Ramtha

September 2011

M	T	W	T	F	S	S
			1	2	3	4
5	6	7	8	9	10	11
12	13	14	15	16	17	18
19	20	21	22	23	24	25
26	27	28	29	30		

Today I am Grateful for . . .

Tuesday 18 October

8 am

10 am

12 pm

2 pm

4 pm

6 pm

		November 2011				
M	T	W	T	F	S	S
	1	2	3	4	5	6
7	8	9	10	11	12	13
14	15	16	17	18	19	20
21	22	23	24	25	26	27
28	29	30				

Today I am Grateful for . . .

Wednesday 19 October

8 am

10 am

12 pm

2 pm

4 pm

6 pm

September 2011

M	T	W	T	F	S	S
			1	2	3	4
5	6	7	8	9	10	11
12	13	14	15	16	17	18
19	20	21	22	23	24	25
26	27	28	29	30		

Today I am Grateful for . . .

Thursday 20 October

8 am

10 am

12 pm

2 pm

4 pm

6 pm

Third Quarter Waning Moon in Cancer
Stay strong and determined to keep the balance within your masculine and feminine self. Where you place your energy is important and will have long-lasting effects.

November 2011

M	T	W	T	F	S	S
	1	2	3	4	5	6
7	8	9	10	11	12	13
14	15	16	17	18	19	20
21	22	23	24	25	26	27
28	29	30				

What do I really Feel about Love?

_____

_____

_____

_____

_____

_____

Friday 21 October

8 am
_____

_____

10 am
_____

_____

12 pm
_____

_____

2 pm
_____

_____

4 pm
_____

_____

6 pm
_____

_____

September 2011						
M	T	W	T	F	S	S
			1	2	3	4
5	6	7	8	9	10	11
12	13	14	15	16	17	18
19	20	21	22	23	24	25
26	27	28	29	30		

Today I am Grateful for . . .

Saturday 22 October

Sunday 23 October

Today I am Grateful for . . .

Monday 24 October

8 am

10 am

12 pm

2 pm

4 pm

6 pm

Age does not protect you from love. But love, to some extent, protects you from age.

Anaïs Nin

September 2011

M	T	W	T	F	S	S
			1	2	3	4
5	6	7	8	9	10	11
12	13	14	15	16	17	18
19	20	21	22	23	24	25
26	27	28	29	30		

Today I am Grateful for . . .

_____

_____

_____

_____

_____

_____

_____

Tuesday 25 October

8 am

_____

_____

10 am

_____

_____

12 pm

_____

_____

2 pm

_____

_____

4 pm

_____

_____

6 pm

_____

_____

November 2011

M	T	W	T	F	S	S
	1	2	3	4	5	6
7	8	9	10	11	12	13
14	15	16	17	18	19	20
21	22	23	24	25	26	27
28	29	30				

Today I am Grateful for . . .

Wednesday 26 October

8 am

10 am

12 pm

2 pm

4 pm

6 pm

		September 2011				
M	T	W	T	F	S	S
			1	2	3	4
5	6	7	8	9	10	11
12	13	14	15	16	17	18
19	20	21	22	23	24	25
26	27	28	29	30		

Today I am Grateful for . . .

○

_____

_____

_____

_____

_____

_____

New or Dark Moon in Scorpio

Thursday 27 October

An intense moon cycle that can bring an amazing sense of hope for the future or a sense of being able to negotiate with those previously not listening. Keep your eye on the image of the best outcome and ask the spirits to guide you.

8 am

_____

10 am

_____

12 pm

_____

2 pm

_____

4 pm

_____

6 pm

_____

November 2011

M	T	W	T	F	S	S
	1	2	3	4	5	6
7	8	9	10	11	12	13
14	15	16	17	18	19	20
21	22	23	24	25	26	27
28	29	30				

Today I am Grateful for . . .

_____

_____

_____

_____

_____

Friday 28 October

8 am

10 am

12 pm

2 pm

4 pm

6 pm

September 2011

M	T	W	T	F	S	S
			1	2	3	4
5	6	7	8	9	10	11
12	13	14	15	16	17	18
19	20	21	22	23	24	25
26	27	28	29	30		

Is my Soul Open to Receiving Love?

Saturday 29 October

Sunday 30 October

Today I am Grateful for ...

_____
_____
_____
_____
_____

Monday 31 October

8 am
_____
_____

10 am
_____
_____

12 pm
_____
_____

2 pm
_____
_____

4 pm
_____
_____

6 pm
_____
_____

Love is reducing the universe down to one being.

Victor Hugo

September 2011

M	T	W	T	F	S	S
			1	2	3	4
5	6	7	8	9	10	11
12	13	14	15	16	17	18
19	20	21	22	23	24	25
26	27	28	29	30		

Reflections on the Month

Community

Gratitude

Photo by Dieter Biskamp

November

If all of us acted in unison as I acted individually, there would be no wars and no poverty. I have made myself personally responsible for the fate of every human being who has come my way.

Anaïs Nin

November 2011

Monday	Tuesday	Wednesday	Thursday	Friday	Saturday	Sunday
	1	2	3	4	5	6
7	8	9	10	11	12	13
14	15	16	17	18	19	20
21	22	23	24	25	26	27
28	29	30				

Today I am Grateful for . . .

Tuesday 1 November

8 am

10 am

12 pm

2 pm

4 pm

6 pm

December 2011

M	T	W	T	F	S	S
			1	2	3	4
5	6	7	8	9	10	11
12	13	14	15	16	17	18
19	20	21	22	23	24	25
26	27	28	29	30	31	

Today I am Grateful for . . .

_____

_____

_____

_____

_____

_____

Wednesday 2 November

8 am

10 am

12 pm

2 pm

4 pm

6 pm

October 2011

M	T	W	T	F	S	S
					1	2
3	4	5	6	7	8	9
10	11	12	13	14	15	16
17	18	19	20	21	22	23
24	25	26	27	28	29	30
31						

Today I am Grateful for . . .

_____
_____
_____
_____
_____
_____
_____

Thursday 3 November

First Quarter Waxing Moon in Aquarius
A little time out to detach else you may allow the tensions to colour your relationships.

8 am

10 am

12 pm

2 pm

4 pm

6 pm

December 2011						
M	T	W	T	F	S	S
			1	2	3	4
5	6	7	8	9	10	11
12	13	14	15	16	17	18
19	20	21	22	23	24	25
26	27	28	29	30	31	

Today I am Grateful for . . .

Friday 4 November

8 am

10 am

12 pm

2 pm

4 pm

6 pm

October 2011

M	T	W	T	F	S	S
					1	2
3	4	5	6	7	8	9
10	11	12	13	14	15	16
17	18	19	20	21	22	23
24	25	26	27	28	29	30
31						

The People I Love . . .

Saturday 5 November

Sunday 6 November

Today I am Grateful for . . .

_____

_____

_____

_____

_____

Monday 7 November

8 am

10 am

12 pm

2 pm

4 pm

6 pm

Love in a civilisation that doesn't consider people equal does not exist. In a civilisation where all people are considered equal—and indeed men and women, regardless of the colour of your skin or eyes, regardless if you are fat or skinny, young or old they should be considered equal—love exists.

Ramtha

Today I am Grateful for . . .

_____
_____
_____
_____
_____
_____

Tuesday 8 November

8 am
_____
_____

10 am
_____
_____

12 pm
_____
_____

2 pm
_____
_____

4 pm
_____
_____

6 pm
_____
_____

December 2011

M	T	W	T	F	S	S
			1	2	3	4
5	6	7	8	9	10	11
12	13	14	15	16	17	18
19	20	21	22	23	24	25
26	27	28	29	30	31	

My Community gives me . . .

_____

_____

_____

_____

_____

Wednesday 9 November

8 am

_____

_____

10 am

_____

_____

12 pm

_____

_____

2 pm

_____

_____

4 pm

_____

_____

6 pm

_____

_____

October 2011						
M	T	W	T	F	S	S
					1	2
3	4	5	6	7	8	9
10	11	12	13	14	15	16
17	18	19	20	21	22	23
24	25	26	27	28	29	30
31						

Today I am Grateful for . . .

_____
_____
_____
_____
_____
_____
_____

Thursday 10 November

8 am
_____
_____

10 am
_____
_____

12 pm
_____
_____

2 pm
_____
_____

4 pm
_____
_____

6 pm
_____
_____

December 2011						
M	T	W	T	F	S	S
			1	2	3	4
5	6	7	8	9	10	11
12	13	14	15	16	17	18
19	20	21	22	23	24	25
26	27	28	29	30	31	

Today I am Grateful for . . .

Friday 11 November

8 am

10 am

12 pm

2 pm

4 pm

6 pm

Full Moon in Taurus
*Give your dreams a voice, a poem, a painting, a piece of music
or a creative collage—spare a moment to express what you most
want to manifest in your life.*

October 2011

M	T	W	T	F	S	S
					1	2
3	4	5	6	7	8	9
10	11	12	13	14	15	16
17	18	19	20	21	22	23
24	25	26	27	28	29	30
31						

Today I am Grateful for . . .

Saturday 12 November

Sunday 13 November

Today I am Grateful for . . .

_____
_____
_____
_____
_____

Monday 14 November

8 am
_____
_____

10 am
_____
_____

12 pm
_____
_____

2 pm
_____
_____

4 pm
_____
_____

6 pm
_____
_____

Imagine, then, a society in which the prevalent legal view
is simply that your brother or your sister is an aspect
of yourself. And if you would help yourself, you must
help them to meet each cry for help and healing with
forgiveness, love, and support. Can you imagine, for a
moment, what it would be like to live in such a society?
How would it be different from the world you see?

			October 2011			
M	T	W	T	F	S	S
					1	2
3	4	5	6	7	8	9
10	11	12	13	14	15	16
17	18	19	20	21	22	23
24	25	26	27	28	29	30
31						

Today I am Grateful for . . .

_____
_____
_____
_____
_____
_____

Tuesday 15 November

8 am
_____
_____

10 am
_____
_____

12 pm
_____
_____

2 pm
_____
_____

4 pm
_____
_____

6 pm
_____
_____

December 2011						
M	T	W	T	F	S	S
			1	2	3	4
5	6	7	8	9	10	11
12	13	14	15	16	17	18
19	20	21	22	23	24	25
26	27	28	29	30	31	

Today I am Grateful for . . .

_____

_____

_____

_____

_____

Wednesday 16 November

8 am

10 am

12 pm

2 pm

4 pm

6 pm

October 2011

M	T	W	T	F	S	S
					1	2
3	4	5	6	7	8	9
10	11	12	13	14	15	16
17	18	19	20	21	22	23
24	25	26	27	28	29	30
31						

My Community . . .

Thursday 17 November

8 am

10 am

12 pm

2 pm

4 pm

6 pm

December 2011

M	T	W	T	F	S	S
			1	2	3	4
5	6	7	8	9	10	11
12	13	14	15	16	17	18
19	20	21	22	23	24	25
26	27	28	29	30	31	

Today I am Grateful for . . .

_____

_____

_____

_____

_____

Friday 18 November

8 am

10 am

12 pm

2 pm

4 pm

6 pm

	October 2011					
M	T	W	T	F	S	S
					1	2
3	4	5	6	7	8	9
10	11	12	13	14	15	16
17	18	19	20	21	22	23
24	25	26	27	28	29	30
31						

Today I am Grateful for . . .

Saturday 19 November

Third Quarter Waning Moon in Leo
Finally you can reap the rewards of this month and breathe a little easier, the hard work is done. The manifestation begins.

Sunday 20 November

Today I am Grateful for . . .

_____

_____

_____

_____

_____

Monday 21 November

8 am

_____

10 am

_____

12 pm

_____

2 pm

_____

4 pm

_____

6 pm

_____

While rugged individualism predisposes one to arrogance, the "soft" individualism of community leads to humility. Begin to appreciate each other's gifts, and you begin to appreciate your own limitations.

M. Scott Peck

October 2011

M	T	W	T	F	S	S
					1	2
3	4	5	6	7	8	9
10	11	12	13	14	15	16
17	18	19	20	21	22	23
24	25	26	27	28	29	30
31						

Today I am Grateful for . . .

Tuesday 22 November

8 am

10 am

12 pm

2 pm

4 pm

6 pm

		December 2011				
M	T	W	T	F	S	S
			1	2	3	4
5	6	7	8	9	10	11
12	13	14	15	16	17	18
19	20	21	22	23	24	25
26	27	28	29	30	31	

I Give my Community . . .

_____

_____

_____

_____

_____

_____

Wednesday 23 November

8 am

10 am

12 pm

2 pm

4 pm

6 pm

October 2011						
M	T	W	T	F	S	S
					1	2
3	4	5	6	7	8	9
10	11	12	13	14	15	16
17	18	19	20	21	22	23
24	25	26	27	28	29	30
31						

Today I am Grateful for . . .

_____
_____
_____
_____
_____
_____
_____

Thursday 24 November

8 am
_____
_____

10 am
_____
_____

12 pm
_____
_____

2 pm
_____
_____

4 pm
_____
_____

6 pm
_____
_____

| December 2011 | | | | | | |
M	T	W	T	F	S	S
			1	2	3	4
5	6	7	8	9	10	11
12	13	14	15	16	17	18
19	20	21	22	23	24	25
26	27	28	29	30	31	

Today I am Grateful for . . .

○

_____
_____
_____
_____
_____

New or Dark Moon in Sagittarius
Solar Eclipse (partial) in 2° Sagittarius
*Symbols and signs light the way. Focus on the smaller details of life
and spend time cleaning up your workspace.*

Friday 25 November

8 am
_____

_____

10 am
_____

_____

12 pm
_____

_____

2 pm
_____

_____

4 pm
_____

_____

6 pm
_____

_____

October 2011

M	T	W	T	F	S	S
					1	2
3	4	5	6	7	8	9
10	11	12	13	14	15	16
17	18	19	20	21	22	23
24	25	26	27	28	29	30
31						

I am Grateful that my Community . . .

Saturday 26 November

Sunday 27 November

Today I am Grateful for . . .

_____

_____

_____

_____

_____

Monday 28 November

8 am
_____

_____

10 am
_____

_____

12 pm
_____

_____

2 pm
_____

_____

4 pm
_____

_____

6 pm
_____

_____

The greatest gift we can give one another is our vulnerability.

Melanie Spears

		October 2011				
M	T	W	T	F	S	S
					1	2
3	4	5	6	7	8	9
10	11	12	13	14	15	16
17	18	19	20	21	22	23
24	25	26	27	28	29	30
31						

Today I am Grateful for . . .

_____

_____

_____

_____

_____

_____

Tuesday 29 November

8 am
_____

_____

10 am
_____

_____

12 pm
_____

_____

2 pm
_____

_____

4 pm
_____

_____

6 pm
_____

_____

December 2011						
M	T	W	T	F	S	S
			1	2	3	4
5	6	7	8	9	10	11
12	13	14	15	16	17	18
19	20	21	22	23	24	25
26	27	28	29	30	31	

I Hold a Vision to one day Live ...

Wednesday 30 November

8 am

10 am

12 pm

2 pm

4 pm

6 pm

	M	T	W	T	F	S	S
						1	2
	3	4	5	6	7	8	9
	10	11	12	13	14	15	16
	17	18	19	20	21	22	23
	24	25	26	27	28	29	30
	31						

October 2011

Reflections on the Month

God

Like two lovers who have become lost in a
winter blizzard
And find a cosy, empty hut in the forest,
I now huddle everywhere with the friend.
God and I have built an immense fire
together
We keep each other happy and warm.

The Subject Tonight is Love, 60 Wild & Sweet Poems of Hafiz,
copyright 1996 and 2003 Daniel Ladinsky and used with his permission.

December

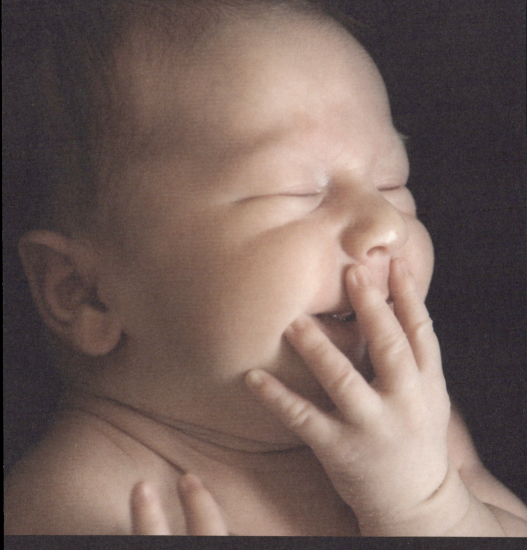

Photo by Andy Glogower

December 2011

Monday	Tuesday	Wednesday	Thursday	Friday	Saturday	Sunday
		1	2	3	4	
5	6	7	8	9	10	11
12	13	14	15	16	17	18
19	20	21	22	23	24	25
26	27	28	29	30	31	

How do I feel about God?

_____

_____

_____

_____

_____

_____

Thursday 1 December

8 am
_____

_____

10 am
_____

_____

12 pm
_____

_____

2 pm
_____

_____

4 pm
_____

_____

6 pm
_____

_____

| January 2012 | | | | | | |
M	T	W	T	F	S	S
						1
2	3	4	5	6	7	8
9	10	11	12	13	14	15
16	17	18	19	20	21	22
23	24	25	26	27	28	29
30	31					

Today I am Grateful for . . .

_____

_____

_____

_____

_____

_____

Friday 2 December

First Quarter Waxing Moon in Pisces
Don't push to get things done—allow. Those all important people skills come in really handy this week. Take time to notice where you could improve when relating with others.

8 am

10 am

12 pm

2 pm

4 pm

6 pm

November 2011

M	T	W	T	F	S	S
	1	2	3	4	5	6
7	8	9	10	11	12	13
14	15	16	17	18	19	20
21	22	23	24	25	26	27
28	29	30				

Today I am Grateful for . . .

Saturday 3 December

Sunday 4 December

Today I am Grateful for . . .

_____

_____

_____

_____

_____

Monday 5 December

8 am
_____

_____

10 am
_____

_____

12 pm
_____

_____

2 pm
_____

_____

4 pm
_____

_____

6 pm
_____

_____

The Law of Attraction is about refining your soul condition to one of two states: The perfection of the NATURAL LOVE path is dependent upon your desire to know yourself. The DIVINE LOVE path is about your desire to know God.

AJ Miller

November 2011

M	T	W	T	F	S	S
	1	2	3	4	5	6
7	8	9	10	11	12	13
14	15	16	17	18	19	20
21	22	23	24	25	26	27
28	29	30				

Am I in a Relationship with God?

_____

_____

_____

_____

_____

_____

Tuesday 6 December

8 am
_____

_____

10 am
_____

_____

12 pm
_____

_____

2 pm
_____

_____

4 pm
_____

_____

6 pm
_____

_____

_____

		January 2012				
M	T	W	T	F	S	S
						1
2	3	4	5	6	7	8
9	10	11	12	13	14	15
16	17	18	19	20	21	22
23	24	25	26	27	28	29
30	31					

God Desires my Love . . .

_____

_____

_____

_____

_____

Wednesday 7 December

8 am
_____

_____

10 am
_____

_____

12 pm
_____

_____

2 pm
_____

_____

4 pm
_____

_____

6 pm
_____

_____

November 2011

M	T	W	T	F	S	S
	1	2	3	4	5	6
7	8	9	10	11	12	13
14	15	16	17	18	19	20
21	22	23	24	25	26	27
28	29	30				

Today I am Grateful for . . .

_____
_____
_____
_____
_____
_____
_____

Thursday 8 December

8 am
_____
_____
_____

10 am
_____
_____
_____

12 pm
_____
_____
_____

2 pm
_____
_____
_____

4 pm
_____
_____
_____

6 pm
_____
_____

January 2012

M	T	W	T	F	S	S
						1
2	3	4	5	6	7	8
9	10	11	12	13	14	15
16	17	18	19	20	21	22
23	24	25	26	27	28	29
30	31					

Today I am Grateful for . . .

Friday 9 December

8 am

10 am

12 pm

2 pm

4 pm

6 pm

November 2011

M	T	W	T	F	S	S
	1	2	3	4	5	6
7	8	9	10	11	12	13
14	15	16	17	18	19	20
21	22	23	24	25	26	27
28	29	30				

Today I am Grateful for . . .

Saturday 10 December

Sunday 11 December

Full Moon in Gemini © **Lunar Eclipse** (total) in 18° Gemini
Where can you soften and give a little? Achieving goals is so much greater when we nurture those we interact with along the way.

Today I am Grateful for . . .

_____

_____

_____

_____

_____

_____

Monday 12 December

8 am
_____

_____

10 am
_____

_____

12 pm
_____

_____

2 pm
_____

_____

4 pm
_____

_____

6 pm
_____

_____

God is a Being or Entity with Attributes and Characteristics. He is not some abstract force without personality, nor is he part of or inside all of his creation. His love can be within any of his children. If God was just a force, without personality, then a personal relationship with God would be impossible.

AJ Miller

November 2011

M	T	W	T	F	S	S
	1	2	3	4	5	6
7	8	9	10	11	12	13
14	15	16	17	18	19	20
21	22	23	24	25	26	27
28	29	30				

Today I am Grateful for . . .

Tuesday 13 December

8 am

---

10 am

---

12 pm

---

2 pm

---

4 pm

---

6 pm

January 2012

M	T	W	T	F	S	S
						1
2	3	4	5	6	7	8
9	10	11	12	13	14	15
16	17	18	19	20	21	22
23	24	25	26	27	28	29
30	31					

Today I am Grateful for . . .

_____

_____

_____

_____

_____

Wednesday 14 December

8 am

_____

10 am

_____

12 pm

_____

2 pm

_____

4 pm

_____

6 pm

_____

_____

		November 2011				
M	T	W	T	F	S	S
	1	2	3	4	5	6
7	8	9	10	11	12	13
14	15	16	17	18	19	20
21	22	23	24	25	26	27
28	29	30				

I am Worthy of Love . . .

_____

_____

_____

_____

_____

_____

Thursday 15 December

8 am

_____

_____

10 am

_____

_____

12 pm

_____

_____

2 pm

_____

_____

4 pm

_____

_____

6 pm

_____

_____

January 2012						
M	T	W	T	F	S	S
						1
2	3	4	5	6	7	8
9	10	11	12	13	14	15
16	17	18	19	20	21	22
23	24	25	26	27	28	29
30	31					

I was Created Perfect . . .

Friday 16 December

8 am

10 am

12 pm

2 pm

4 pm

6 pm

November 2011

M	T	W	T	F	S	S
	1	2	3	4	5	6
7	8	9	10	11	12	13
14	15	16	17	18	19	20
21	22	23	24	25	26	27
28	29	30				

Today I am Grateful for ...

Saturday 17 December

Sunday 18 December

Third Quarter Waning Moon in Virgo
OK, that's it! Time to get moving. Finalising those outstanding details will come more easily now. With a no frills attitude communications flow—the power is in the giving whilst being true to yourself. Get on with it.

Today I am Grateful for . . .

Monday 19 December

8 am

10 am

12 pm

2 pm

4 pm

6 pm

Prayer is like a deep desire to know God well, as a friend, to understand his/her feelings and emotions.

AJ Miller

November 2011

M	T	W	T	F	S	S
	1	2	3	4	5	6
7	8	9	10	11	12	13
14	15	16	17	18	19	20
21	22	23	24	25	26	27
28	29	30				

Do I Receive God's Love?

_____

_____

_____

_____

_____

_____

Tuesday 20 December

8 am

_____

_____

10 am

_____

_____

12 pm

_____

_____

2 pm

_____

_____

4 pm

_____

_____

6 pm

_____

_____

January 2012						
M	T	W	T	F	S	S
						1
2	3	4	5	6	7	8
9	10	11	12	13	14	15
16	17	18	19	20	21	22
23	24	25	26	27	28	29
30	31					

Do I feel Worthy of Love?

_____
_____
_____
_____
_____
_____

Wednesday 21 December

8 am
_____
_____

10 am
_____
_____

12 pm
_____
_____

2 pm
_____
_____

4 pm
_____
_____

6 pm
_____
_____

		November 2011				
M	T	W	T	F	S	S
	1	2	3	4	5	6
7	8	9	10	11	12	13
14	15	16	17	18	19	20
21	22	23	24	25	26	27
28	29	30				

Today I am Grateful for . . .

_____

_____

_____

_____

_____

_____

Thursday 22 December

8 am

December Solstice
*Where do you place your power and how do you help to empower others?
Relationships can come under stress as intense transformational energy
is unleashed. Allow those who inspire you help you choose a path of
compassion and honesty.*

10 am

12 pm

2 pm

4 pm

6 pm

January 2012

M	T	W	T	F	S	S
						1
2	3	4	5	6	7	8
9	10	11	12	13	14	15
16	17	18	19	20	21	22
23	24	25	26	27	28	29
30	31					

Today I am Grateful for . . .

Friday 23 December

8 am

---

10 am

---

12 pm

---

2 pm

---

4 pm

---

6 pm

November 2011						
M	T	W	T	F	S	S
	1	2	3	4	5	6
7	8	9	10	11	12	13
14	15	16	17	18	19	20
21	22	23	24	25	26	27
28	29	30				

Today I am Grateful for . . .

◯

Saturday 24 December

New or Dark Moon in Capricorn
A New Moon on Christmas day. A quieter non-traditional gathering with those who accept you as you are will be the most joyous expression of this energy.

Sunday 25 December

Today I am Grateful for . . .

_____

_____

_____

_____

_____

_____

Monday 26 December

8 am

_____

_____

10 am

_____

_____

12 pm

_____

_____

2 pm

_____

_____

4 pm

_____

_____

6 pm

_____

_____

We are yet to fully know how much God has done in Her
desire for us to experience Her Love. God is deserving of
all the Glory and the honor our finite souls can give.

AJ Miller

November 2011

M	T	W	T	F	S	S
	1	2	3	4	5	6
7	8	9	10	11	12	13
14	15	16	17	18	19	20
21	22	23	24	25	26	27
28	29	30				

Today I am Grateful for . . .

_____

_____

_____

_____

_____

_____

Tuesday 27 December

8 am

_____

_____

10 am

_____

_____

12 pm

_____

_____

2 pm

_____

_____

4 pm

_____

_____

6 pm

_____

_____

_____

January 2012

M	T	W	T	F	S	S
						1
2	3	4	5	6	7	8
9	10	11	12	13	14	15
16	17	18	19	20	21	22
23	24	25	26	27	28	29
30	31					

Do I feel worthy of God's love?

Wednesday 28 December

8 am

10 am

12 pm

2 pm

4 pm

6 pm

		November 2011				
M	T	W	T	F	S	S
	1	2	3	4	5	6
7	8	9	10	11	12	13
14	15	16	17	18	19	20
21	22	23	24	25	26	27
28	29	30				

Today I am Grateful for . . .

_____

_____

_____

_____

_____

_____

_____

Thursday 29 December

8 am

_____

_____

10 am

_____

_____

12 pm

_____

_____

2 pm

_____

_____

4 pm

_____

_____

6 pm

_____

_____

		January 2012				
M	T	W	T	F	S	S
						1
2	3	4	5	6	7	8
9	10	11	12	13	14	15
16	17	18	19	20	21	22
23	24	25	26	27	28	29
30	31					

Today I am Grateful for ...

_____

_____

_____

_____

_____

Friday 30 December

8 am
_____

_____

10 am
_____

_____

12 pm
_____

_____

2 pm
_____

_____

4 pm
_____

_____

6 pm
_____

_____

		November 2011				
M	T	W	T	F	S	S
	1	2	3	4	5	6
7	8	9	10	11	12	13
14	15	16	17	18	19	20
21	22	23	24	25	26	27
28	29	30				

Today I am Grateful for . . .

Saturday 31 December

If I could be any part of you,
I'd be your tears.
To be conceived in your heart,
born in your eyes,
live on your cheeks,
and die on your lips. . .
Author unknown

Reflections on the Month

Reflections on the Year

Address Book—A B C D

Name:	Home:
Address:	Work
	Fax:
Email:	Mob:

Name:	Home:
Address:	Work
	Fax:
Email:	Mob:

Name:	Home:
Address:	Work
	Fax:
Email:	Mob:

Name:	Home:
Address:	Work
	Fax:
Email:	Mob:

Name:	Home:
Address:	Work
	Fax:
Email:	Mob:

Name:	Home:
Address:	Work
	Fax:
Email:	Mob:

Name:	Home:
Address:	Work
	Fax:
Email:	Mob:

Address Book—E F G H

Name:	Home:
Address:	Work
	Fax:
Email:	Mob:
Name:	Home:
Address:	Work
	Fax:
Email:	Mob:
Name:	Home:
Address:	Work
	Fax:
Email:	Mob:
Name:	Home:
Address:	Work
	Fax:
Email:	Mob:
Name:	Home:
Address:	Work
	Fax:
Email:	Mob:
Name:	Home:
Address:	Work
	Fax:
Email:	Mob:
Name:	Home:
Address:	Work
	Fax:
Email:	Mob:

Address Book—I J K L

Name:	Home:
Address:	Work
	Fax:
Email:	Mob:
Name:	Home:
Address:	Work
	Fax:
Email:	Mob:
Name:	Home:
Address:	Work
	Fax:
Email:	Mob:
Name:	Home:
Address:	Work
	Fax:
Email:	Mob:
Name:	Home:
Address:	Work
	Fax:
Email:	Mob:
Name:	Home:
Address:	Work
	Fax:
Email:	Mob:
Name:	Home:
Address:	Work
	Fax:
Email:	Mob:

Address Book—M N O P

Name:	Home:
Address:	Work
	Fax:
Email:	Mob:
Name:	Home:
Address:	Work
	Fax:
Email:	Mob:
Name:	Home:
Address:	Work
	Fax:
Email:	Mob:
Name:	Home:
Address:	Work
	Fax:
Email:	Mob:
Name:	Home:
Address:	Work
	Fax:
Email:	Mob:
Name:	Home:
Address:	Work
	Fax:
Email:	Mob:
Name:	Home:
Address:	Work
	Fax:
Email:	Mob:

Address Book—Q R S T U

Name:	Home:
Address:	Work
	Fax:
Email:	Mob:
Name:	Home:
Address:	Work
	Fax:
Email:	Mob:
Name:	Home:
Address:	Work
	Fax:
Email:	Mob:
Name:	Home:
Address:	Work
	Fax:
Email:	Mob:
Name:	Home:
Address:	Work
	Fax:
Email:	Mob:
Name:	Home:
Address:	Work
	Fax:
Email:	Mob:
Name:	Home:
Address:	Work
	Fax:
Email:	Mob:

Address Book—V W X Y Z

Name:	Home:
Address:	Work
	Fax:
Email:	Mob:

Name:	Home:
Address:	Work
	Fax:
Email:	Mob:

Name:	Home:
Address:	Work
	Fax:
Email:	Mob:

Name:	Home:
Address:	Work
	Fax:
Email:	Mob:

Name:	Home:
Address:	Work
	Fax:
Email:	Mob:

Name:	Home:
Address:	Work
	Fax:
Email:	Mob:

Name:	Home:
Address:	Work
	Fax:
Email:	Mob:

2012 Yearly Planner

January	February	March
1	1	1
2	2	2
3	3	3
4	4	4
5	5	5
6	6	6
7	7	7
8	8	8
9	9	9
10	10	10
11	11	11
12	12	12
13	13	13
14	14	14
15	15	15
16	16	16
17	17	17
18	18	18
19	19	19
20	20	20
21	21	21
22	22	22
23	23	23
24	24	24
25	25	25
26	26	26
27	27	27
28	28	28
29		29
30		30
31		31

For your convenience
take advantage of our easy mail order service

Title	Cost	Number	Total
2011 Gratitude Diary and Daily Planner	$33.00		
2012 Gratitude Diary and Daily Planner	$33.00		
P&H 1diary: **$12.50**			
P&H 10–15 diaries: **$18**			
TOTAL			

Name:

Address:

Suburb:

State/Province: Postcode/Zip:

Country:

Phone:

Fax:

Email:

Please send orders to:
Gratitude Diary
PO Box 31
Ocean Shores, NSW 2483
Australia

WEBSITE: www.diarygratitude.com